LAND

RENTON

The Royal Court Writers Series
published by Methuen
in association with the Royal Court Theatre

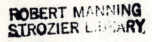
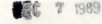
METHUEN'S NEW THEATRESCRIPTS

First published as a paperback original in 1988 by Methuen Drama,
Michelin House, 81 Fulham Road, London SW3 6RB

Copyright © 1988 by Howard Brenton.

British Library Cataloguing in Publication Data

    Brenton, Howard, 1942-
        Greenland.———(The Royal Court writers series).
        I. Title   II. Series
        822'.914

        ISBN 0-413-19530-9

Printed in Great Britain by Expression Printers Ltd, London N7

3 PLAYS FOR UTOPIA
A Howard Brenton Season
On Writing the Utopian Plays

"I first had the idea of writing a 'Utopian' play eleven years ago. I was on Epsom racecourse at the Derby of 1977 (Piggot on The Minstrel). It was one of those far-fetched ideas that can come to a playwright on a glorious summer's day — and then take ten years to finally achieve.

My first attempt at a play with Utopian themes was SORE THROATS (1978 RSC at the Warehouse Theatre). It begins far from human dignity and peace. The first act is the most violent writing I have ever done. My instinct was that if you are going to show people moving towards a transformation into citizens of a Utopia or, in SORE THROATS, a Utopian state of mind, you have to show them first at their vilest and their most uphappy. A playwright who shirks from writing about people at their worst, will not be believed when trying to write about them at their best. The three characters in SORE THROATS set out on a crazy voyage in the play's second act. I finally imagined where to in the new play of this season, GREENLAND.

After SORE THROATS I attempted an adaptation of William Morris's novel NEWS FROM NOWHERE. This has the reputation of being one of the great loony books of the left. I found it less silly that it is meant to be. But I couldn't make it work. MORRIS wrote in an historical innocence that we do not have. Then I tried a straight forward text, set a thousand years from now. It was incomprehensible. It was also unlivable — in trying to describe a heaven on earth, I had described a hell. I despaired of the idea and burnt everything I'd written for it (my small garden is rich with the typing paper ash of abandoned Utopias — at least they help the runner beans grow.)

Then Roland Rees of Foco Novo Theatre asked me to write a play about the poet Shelley. What interested me about Shelley, Byron and their circle was that they were would-be Utopians, not only in their work and their views, but in the way they tried to live. So the play about them, BLOODY POETRY (1984, Foco Novo Theatre, Leicester Haymarket and Hampstead Theatre), was a window opening for me. Byron, Shelley, Mary and Claire are moderns. They belong to us. They suffered exile from a reactionary, mean England, of which ours in the 1980s is an echo. They were defeated, they also behaved, at times, abominably to each other. But I wrote BLOODY POETRY to celebrate and to salute them. Whether they really failed in their 'Utopian dreams' is not yet resolved.

In GREENLAND I come clean. Over half the play is set seven hundred years in the future. I have tried to dramatise how I hope my children, or my children's children's children, will live and think. The 'Greenlanders' in the play are strange, and their sense of humour is disturbing, but I would love to meet them.

Howard Brenton

Shelley said to me, when
I asked for a tip, 'Write first
For a new world within —
Always of
Men, women, nature and society —
Never forget
The world is old
But its great age has yet
To be made
Let alone told —
And declare you are a public enemy
Of kingly death, false beauty and decay'
Ta, Percy. I'm on my way

(*Sonnet 30 from* SONNETS OF LOVE AND OPPOSITION BY HOWARD BRENTON)

COMING NEXT

IN THE MAIN HOUSE 730 1745

From 21 July

THE RECRUITING OFFICER

by George Farquhar
Directed by Max Stafford-Clark

Farquhar's classic comedy in its first major London production since 1963. Set in Shrewsbury in 1706, it gives a vivid, colourful and fascinating picture of small town life and charts the desire of two determined young women to bring their lovers to heel. At the same time, Captain Plume and Sergeant Kite launch a major recruiting drive.

From 1st September

OUR COUNTRY'S GOOD

by Timberlake Wertenbaker
based on Thomas Keneally's novel *The Playmaker*.
Directed by Max Stafford-Clark

The Recruiting Officer company will also be seen in Timberlake Wertenbaker's new play. Set in the convict colony perched on the rim of Australia in 1789, a young marine lieutenant directs a group of convicts through the rehearsals and production of *The Recruiting Officer*. Rehearsals are threatened — it's possible that the leading lady may be hanged, the colony's priest fears the production will be an incitement to immorality and the director has bad dreams.

IN THE THEATRE UPSTAIRS 730 2554

June 3-25

THE ROYAL COURT YOUNG PEOPLES' THEATRE

presents

THE RANK XEROX/ROYAL COURT YOUNG WRITERS' FESTIVAL

Directors: Phyllida Lloyd, Tim Supple

This year, for the first time ever, Royal Court writers and directors have led Writers' Workshops for young people all over the country. From this, a wealth of exciting new talent has been discovered expressing the concerns of young people as they approach the 1990's. The selected plays are *Lalita's Way* by 19 year old Soraya Jintan; *The Burrow* by 21 year old Hannah Vincent and *Mohair* by 21 year old Jonathan Harvey. There will also be a programme of Festival Extras which will vary each evening.

THE YOUNG WRITERS' FESTIVAL will tour to the writers' local regions:

Theatre Royal and Opera House, Wakefield: 28th June - 2nd July
Spring Street Theatre, Hull: 5th - 9th July
Mercury Theatre Studio, Colchester: 12th - 16th July

From 7 July

DOWNFALL

by Gregory Motton
Directed by Lindsay Posner

There is murder, longing and revolution in the City as the searchlights cut through the dark, dark night: a brilliant array of characters breaks from the shadows.

Gregory Motton's daring new play is a Royal Court commission and follows *Ambulance* seen UPSTAIRS in 1987.

"Beneath the jokes and punkish swagger it is a young voice of urban displacement and unlocated grief." Michael Ratcliffe, THE OBSERVER.

AT THE ROYAL COURT

For the last three years the Royal Court has had to supplement its box office earnings and government grants with fund-raising from private business sources. While we have been relatively successful in meeting our fundraising targets and recent years have seen better and better earnings from the box office, the future looks as difficult as ever, in spite of the Arts Minister's announcement of a three-year increase in the Arts Council's grant-in-aid. Increasingly, therefore, the Royal Court needs a body of regular support in its fundraising drive and so we are introducing our new patronage scheme. For many years now Members of the Royal Court Theatre Society have received special notice of new productions and priority booking, but why not consider contributing £35 (or £50 joint membership) and become a **Friend of the Royal Court** — or approach your company or business to become an **Associate** or a **Patron**, thereby involving yourself directly in maintaining the high standard and unique quality of Royal Court productions — while enjoying complimentary tickets to the shows themselves?

1 MEMBERSHIP SCHEME

For £10 you will receive details of all forthcoming events via the Royal Court *Member's Letter*; be given priority booking at the box office and be entitled to purchase any available seat for £3 during previews (maximum of two per Member).

2 FRIENDS
OF THE ROYAL COURT

For £35 (or £50 joint membership) you will be entitled to one (or two) complimentary preview ticket(s) for performances on the Main Stage and one (or two) exchange vouchers for productions in the Theatre Upstairs. You will automatically be on our mailing list and be invited to all lectures and special events.

3 ASSOCIATES
OF THE ROYAL COURT

For £350 you will be entitled to two top priority tickets (previews or press nights) to all Main House productions, two tickets to all plays in the Theatre Upstairs and priority block ticket-booking availability. You will also be invited to a special Associates lunch on stage and also the Annual Associates Cocktail Party/Lecture. If desired, you can appear in the Royal Court programme and be presented with a certificate stating your membership of this exclusive club.

4 INDIVIDUAL PATRONS

For £1,000 you can make a 'personal appearance' on a plaque in the Royal Court lobby, appear in our programme and be invited to a special glittering event. In addition, you will be entitled to ten free tickets for five shows in the Main House or the Theatre Upstairs.

When you have chosen from the four categories, please make your cheque/P.O. payable to the *Royal Court Theatre Society* and send to: *Max Stafford-Clark, Artistic Director, Royal Court Theatre, Sloane Square, London SW1*. Alternatively, if you wish to covenant for four years or more by filling in the form which you will find in the theatre foyer, we — as a registered charity — can claim back the tax you have already paid, thereby increasing the value of your donation.

PATRONS

Henny Gestetner

ASSOCIATES

John Arthur, Richard Barran, Michael Codron, Patricia Marmont, David Mirvish, Sir Dermot de Trafford.

FRIENDS

Jim Broadbent, Ralph Brown, Paul Sinclair Brooks, Carol Bush, Guy Chapman, Michael Codron, Angela Coles, C. Collingwood, Jeremy Conway, Lou Coulson, Alan David, Ann Diamond, R. H. & B. H. Dowler, William & Libby Duffy, Adrian Charles Dunbar, Dolores Edwardes, Jan Evans, Trevor Eve, Kenneth Ewing, Kate Feast, Rachel Feuchtwang, Gilly Fraser, Kerry Gardner, Mrs. Graham, Hamper-Neafsey Associates, Jocelyn Herbert, Dusty Hughes, Kenny Ireland, Paul Jesson, Alex King, Sheila Lemon, London Arts Discovery Tours, Philip MacDonald, Suzie MacKenzie, Barbara Mackie, Marina Martin, Alfred Molina, Alex Nash, Richard O'Brian, Sophie Sky Okonedu, Stephen Oliver, Gary Olsen, Harold Pinter, Margaret Ramsay, Alan Rickman, P. A. Rixon, A. J. Sayers, Louise Stein, Lindsay Stevens & Glen Berelowitz, Richard Stone, Nigel Terry, Mary Trevelyan, Tracey Ullman, Julian Wadham, Julia Walter, Richard Wilson.

THE ROYAL COURT THEATRE
presents

GREENLAND

by
Howard Brenton

Cast in order of appearance
ACT ONE
— US —

JOAN	Jane Lapotaire
BILL	Ben Onwukwe
POLICEMAN	Larry Lamb
BETTY BLAZE	Sheila Hancock
SISTER ANNE } Evangelists	Janet McTeer
BROTHER GEORGE	David Haig
ROGER, A Reporter	Ron Cook
MARY	Jane Lapotaire
CENTURION	Ben Onwukwe
JUDY, Betty's Daughter	Lesley Sharp
BRIAN	Larry Lamb
DOT, Brian's Sister	Sheila Hancock
PAUL, LORD LUDLOW	David Haig
MILLY, Paul's Wife	Janet McTeer
VAL	Lesley Sharp
JACKO	Ron Cook
ANDREW } Paul's Friends	Ben Onwukwe
HUGH	Larry Lamb
DON	Ron Cook
JEFF	David Haig
BUSKER	Carol Sloman

ACT TWO
— THEM —

DRAW	} Beachcombers	Ron Cook
A'BET		Lesley Sharp

JACE, A Jeweller .... Ben Onwukwe

SIU .... Janet McTeer

ANNETTE, An Archaeologist .... Lesley Sharp

SASHA, Her Assistant .... Ron Cook

OH'		Ben Onwukwe
LAI FUNG	} Lovers	Lesley Sharp
SALLY		Janet McTeer

SEVERAN-SEVERAN, An Historian .... Ron Cook

PALACE, A Nurse .... Janet McTeer

GREENLANDER .... Carol Sloman

Directed by	Simon Curtis
Designed by	Paul Brown
Lighting by	Andy Phillips
Music by	Stephen Warbeck
Sound by	Christopher Shutt
Fight Arranger	Terry King
Costume Supervisor	Katie Birrell
Assistant Director	Philip Howard
Stage Manager	Gemma Bodley
Deputy Stage Manager	Fiona Bardsley
Assistant Stage Manager	Suzy Stamp
Poster Design	2D Design
Production Photographs	John Haynes

Musical Instruments made by Simon Levy, Veena Stephenson,
Stephen Warbeck, Angus Watt, Graham Westfield, with
Andrew Dickson, Christopher Shutt, Robert Wood.

THERE WILL BE ONE INTERVAL OF FIFTEEN MINUTES

PAUL BROWN - Trained under Margaret Harris at Riverside Studios; for the Royal Court: *1985 YOUNG WRITERS' FESTIVAL, Ourselves Alone, Road, A Lie of the Mind.*

RON COOK - Theatre work includes: *Sons of Light, Television Times, The Winter's Tale, The Crucible, The Dillen* (RSC), *She Stoops to Conquer* (Lyric Hammersmith); *Ecstasy* and *How I Got That Story* (Hampstead); *Cock-Ups* (Royal Exchange, Manchester); *Three Sisters* (Greenwich/Albery); for the Royal Court: *The Arbor, Cloud Nine, The Grass Widow.* TV includes: title role in *Richard III, Henry VI* parts 1, 2 and 3, *The Merry Wives of Windsor, A Day to Remember, The Singing Detective, The Miser, Bergerac, Les Girls.*

SIMON CURTIS - Trained as Max Stafford-Clark's Assistant, before directing *Deadlines, 1985 YOUNG WRITERS' FESTIVAL,* Anne Devlin's *Ourselves Alone,* Jim Cartwright's *Road, Royal Borough* and *A Lie of the Mind* by Sam Shepard. Nominated 1986 Olivier Awards Most Promising Newcomer and is the Deputy Director of the Royal Court. This summer is directing *Road* at the Lincoln Center, New York.

DAVID HAIG - For the Royal Court: *1980 YOUNG WRITERS' FESTIVAL, The Arbor, Care, Tom and Viv,* (London and New York); for the RSC: *A Midsummer Night's Dream, Volpone, Every Man in His Humour, Worlds Apart, Time of Your Life.* TV includes: *Flame to the Phoenix, Chessgame, Diamonds, Dr. Who, Moonstallion, Blake's Seven.* Films include: *Morons from Outer Space.* Radio includes: *Howard's End, Day Out, Men.*

SHEILA HANCOCK - Recent Theatre: *Sweeney Todd* (Drury Lane); *Peter Pan* and *The Winter's Tale* (RSC); *The Duchess of Malfi* and *The Cherry Orchard* (National Theatre). Recent TV includes: *The Rivals,* and *Jumping the Queue.* Films include: *Hawks* and *Buster.* As a director: Associate Artistic Director of Cambridge Theatre Company; *A Midsummer Night's Dream* (RSC) and Artistic Director RSC Small Scale Tour 1984; *The Critic* (National Theatre). A director of the Actors' Centre. Book: *Ramblings of an Actress* (1988). Received OBE in 1974.

LARRY LAMB - Theatre includes Filumena (Lyric); *Seduced* and *Insignificance* (Royal Court); *Comedians* (Broadway). TV includes: *Fox, Jemima Shore Investigates, The World Walk, Christopher Columbus, Shadey, Boon, Slip Up, Harry's Kingdom, The Two Brothers.* Films include: *Americonga, Underworld, Hearts of Fire* and *Buster.*

JANE LAPOTAIRE - Recent Theatre includes: *Piaf* (RSC/West End/Broadway - several awards), *Misalliance* and *Archbishop's Ceiling* (RSC); *Saint Joan* (Compass); *L'Aide Memoire* (Theatre Artaud at French Institute). TV includes: *Marie Curie* (BAFTA and Emmy nominations), *Anthony and Cleopatra*, *Lady Macbeth*, *Radical Chambers*. Films include: *Lady Jane*, *Napoleon and Josephine*.

JANET McTEER - Theatre includes: *A Midsummer Night's Dream* and *Worlds Apart* (RSC); *As You Like It*, *Three Sisters*, *Cymbeline* (Royal Exchange, Manchester); for the Royal Court: *The Grace of Mary Traverse*. TV includes: *Les Girls* and *Miss Julie*. Films include *Hawks*.

BEN ONWUKWE - Theatre includes: *Trojans* (Black Theatre Co-op), *Othello* (Roundhouse), *Scrape Off the Black* (Temba), *Smile Orange* (Theatre Royal, Stratford East), *Blood Brothers* (London Bubble tour), *Hamlet* (Chaucer Theatre), *Pink Briefcase* (Lyric Hammersmith), *Andromache* (Old Vic); for the Royal Court: *The Emperor* (also TV). Other TV includes: *Slingers Day*. Films include: *The Chain*.

ANDY PHILLIPS - Was resident lighting designer at the Royal Court 1965-1972, where he lit over 80 productions; other lighting designs for the Royal Court include: *Women Beware Women*, *Rat in the Skull*, The Edward Bond Season and, most recently, *The Last Supper*. He designed the lighting for John Dexter's production of *M Butterfly*, currently on Broadway.

LESLEY SHARP - Theatre includes: *Macbeth*, *Maydays*, *Lear* (RSC); *Six Characters in Search of An Author*, *Fathers and Sons*, *Ting Tang Mine*, *True Dare Kiss*, *Command or Promise* (National Theatre); *A Family Affair* (Cheek by Jowl); for the Royal Court: *Road* and *Shirley*. TV includes: *Road*, *Tartuffe*, *The World of UB40*. Films include: *Rita, Sue and Bob Too* and *The Love Child*.

CAROL SLOMAN - Theatre includes: *Lennon* (Astoria - 1985 Olivier nomination), *The Threepenny Opera* (Duke's Playhouse, Lancaster), *Ram Alley* (Contact Theatre, Manchester), *Who Cares* (tour); for the Royal Court: *A Lie of the Mind*. Has composed music for: *Shadow of a Doubt* and *Crazy* (Avon Touring Company); *Aladdin* and *Jack and the Beanstalk* (Duke's Playhouse, Lancaster); *Mamma Mia* (tour).

STEPHEN WARBECK - has composed music for: *The Caucasian Chalk Circle* (Oxford Playhouse and Thames TV), *Soft Soap* and *A Woman Alone* (BBC), *The Good Person of Szechuan*, *The Comedy of Errors*; for the Royal Court: *Built on Sand*, *Royal Borough*, *A Lie of the Mind*, *Bloody Poetry*; musical director for *The Mother* (National Theatre). Other theatre includes: Hull Truck, Glasgow Citizens, Manchester Royal Exchange, Young Vic, Liverpool Playhouse, Liverpool Everyman, Theatre Royal Stratford East.

FOR THE ROYAL COURT

DIRECTION

Artistic Director . . . . MAX STAFFORD-CLARK
Deputy Director . . . . SIMON CURTIS
Director of the Theatre Upstairs . . . . LINDSAY POSNER
Assistant Director . . . . PHILIP HOWARD
Casting Director . . . . LISA MAKIN
Literary Manager . . . . KATE HARWOOD
Senior Script Associate . . . . MICHAEL HASTINGS*
Resident Playwright . . . . HARWANT S. BAINS*
Artistic Assistant . . . . MELANIE KENYON

PRODUCTION

Production Manager . . . . BO BARTON
Technical Manager, Theatre Upstairs . . . . CHRIS BAGUST
Chief Electrician . . . . CHRISTOPHER TOULMIN
Deputy Chief Electrician . . . . MARK BRADLEY
Electrician . . . . COLIN ROXBOROUGH*
Sound Designer . . . . CHRISTOPHER SHUTT
Master Carpenter . . . . CHRIS HARDING-ROBERTS
Deputy Carpenter . . . . JOHN BURGESS
Costume Supervisor . . . . JENNIFER COOK
Wardrobe Assistants . . . . IONA KENRICK*, CATHIE SKILBECK

ADMINISTRATION

General Manager . . . . GRAHAM COWLEY
Assistant to General Manager . . . . LUCY WOOLLATT
Finance Administrator . . . . STEPHEN MORRIS
Finance Assistant . . . . GILL RUSSELL
Press Manager . . . . SALLY LYCETT
Publicity & Marketing Manager . . . . GUY CHAPMAN
Development Director . . . . TOM PETZAL
Development Assistant . . . . JACQUELINE VIEIRA
House Manager . . . . GODFREY HAMILTON
Assistant House Manager . . . . ALISON SMITH
Bookshop Manager . . . . DIANE PETHERICK*
Box Office Manager . . . . STEVEN CURRIE
Box Office Assistant . . . . GERALD BROOKING
Stage Door/Telephonists . . . . DIANE PETHERICK*, ANGELA TOULMIN*
Evening Stage Door . . . . TYRONE LUCAS*, CERI SHIELDS*
Maintenance . . . . JOHN LORRIGIO*
Cleaners . . . . EILEEN CHAPMAN*, IVY JONES*
Firemen . . . . MICK BROWN*, PAUL KLEINMANN*

YOUNG PEOPLE'S THEATRE

Director . . . . ELYSE DODGSON
Administrator . . . . JANE HELLINGS
Youth Drama Worker . . . . SUZY GILMOUR
Schools & Comunity Liaison Worker . . . . MARK HOLNESS
Writer in Residence . . . . KARIM ALRAWI*

*Part-time staff

COUNCIL:Chairman: MATTHEW EVANS, CHRIS BAGUST, BO BARTON, STUART BURGE, ANTHONY C. BURTON, CARYL CHURCHILL, BRIAN COX, HARRIET CRUICKSHANK, SIMON CURTIS, ALLAN DAVIS, DAVID LLOYD DAVIS, ROBERT FOX, MRS. HENNY GESTETNER OBE, DEREK GRANGER, DAVID HARE, JOCELYN HERBERT, DAVID KLEEMAN, HANIF KUREISHI, SONIA MELCHETT, JOAN PLOWRIGHT CBE, GREVILLE POKE, JANE RAYNE, JIM TANNER, SIR HUGH WILLATT.

THIS THEATRE IS ASSOCIATED WITH THE THAMES TELEVISION PLAYWRIGHT SCHEME AND THE REGIONAL THEATRE YOUNG DIRECTORS SCHEME.

GREENLAND

To Wolfgang Lippke

'We're here to build cathedrals'
Joseph Beuys

Notes

To be performed by a company of four men and four women.

The action of the play takes place on 11 June 1987, and 700 years from then.

ACT ONE

Scene One

Lights up.

7 a.m. Thursday, 11 June, 1987.

JOAN *there. She is dressed in a well cut coat. 'Good' shoes. She wears a large Labour Party rosette.*

JOAN. Mum? Dad?

Today your daughter will be elected to the House of Commons.

Yup! Your Joan, your Joanie, is going to change the world.

A laugh to herself. A pause.

You'd have been proud. Even you Dad, you old Stalinist. If only you were here.

Straightens.

Right! The only time today you think like that, my girl!

BILL *comes on, fast. He carries three clipboards, loaded with papers, a bulging briefcase, and three large electric megaphones. He too wears a large Labour Party rosette.*

BILL. The turn out at the committee rooms is great. A lot of helpers.

JOAN. I saw Punk Eddie hanging around the Park Grove committee room. Bill! Now keep him and his lot off the street.

BILL. Punk Eddie is dead keen . . .

JOAN. Bill! I am not going to have a mad Glaswegian with red eyes and a green, three foot high Mohican haircut, knocking on doors telling people to vote Labour.

Not today. Today we get it right. Today we are going to win.

BILL. OK.

They look at each other. They grin. Then BILL looks at his watch.

The polls opened. Just then.

JOAN. Let's go.

Walking off together. JOAN talking fast.

I'll go out with the megaphone van at ten.

I'll do Safeway's Shopping Mall at lunchtime. And we'll have the first check of the turnout at twelve, then every two hours. What about drivers and cars for the old folks?

BILL. Tremendous . . .

They are off.

Scene Two

Noon. South London. Outside a school. A cardboard sign – 'Polling Station'.

A young POLICE CONSTABLE stands, hands behind his back. He claps his hands. He blows into each glove at the wrist. Then he looks one way, then the other. Feeling unseen, he quickly gives his balls a scratch. Then he puts his hands behind his back again.

BETTY BLAZE *comes on. She is in her early sixties. She wears a sensible plastic mackintosh and a flamboyant hat with feathers and fruit. She carries a copy of the 'Daily Telegraph'.*

She opens the 'Daily Telegraph'. She kneels on it, in prayer.

BETTY. Oh Lord Jesus. I kneel down in a dirty street of London. For I would see thy Angel with burning sword, oh Lord. A sword of light.

The CONSTABLE starts, is about to move forward. Then he recognises BETTY.

CONSTABLE (*aside*). My God. It is. It's her.

BETTY. Let darkness not fall in England, on this thy sweet land.

For I would that all were praise, over all the roofs, all the gardens, the houses, yea high in the tower blocks and on the motorways, praise, yea in the churches, in the dens of iniquity, in the discos, the strip clubs, all praise, yea even in the studios of the BBC, hallelujah.

For my heart is heavy, sweet Jesus.

Suddenly cross. She looks at her watch.

Well, where are they? I do hate things not happening when people say. Oh, whoops, sorry Lord!

Finishing the prayer off.

For my heart is heavy and thine is the kingdom, the power and the glory, amen.

She snaps out of the prayer. Stands. Picks up the 'Daily Telegraph'. Puts it in her copious handbag and turns to the CONSTABLE *with a beaming smile.*

Good morning Officer!

He nods.

BETTY. I hope the voters are flocking!

CONSTABLE. Bit quiet so far, but . .

BETTY *interrupting*.

BETTY. And voting the right way!

CONSTABLE. Well as I see it . . .

BETTY. The Devil does his work, even on Polling Day.

Both of them looking one way, then the other. Nothing happens.

BETTY *looks at her watch.*

BETTY. Really! I know they are the South London anti-pornography committee and good souls, but why can't God's people . . . keep to a timetable?

Two local christians come on, 'SISTER' ANNE and 'BROTHER' GEORGE.

SISTER ANNE. There she is, bless her.

BROTHER GEORGE. Mrs Blaze!

BETTY *glances at them.*

BETTY (*aside*). Oh no, they are amateurs. I can always tell. Give me patience oh Lord, in thy hiding place.

BROTHER GEORGE. What a hat.

SISTER ANNE (*aside*). She's famous for her hats. Amongst the crowds, the TV cameras, photographers from the newspapers, demonstrators – the hat. She said once: 'When I do battle for the Lord, I like a harvest festival on my head.' (*To* BETTY.) What a wonderful hat, Mrs Blaze.

BETTY. Oh thank you dear. When I do battle for the Lord, I like a harvest festival on my head.

SISTER ANNE. But you've said that before . . .

BETTY. Any gentlemen of the press?

BROTHER GEORGE. I telephoned the Methodist Recorder.

BETTY. Yes. Well. That will strike fear into Satan's hoards.

BROTHER GEORGE *is nonplussed.* BETTY *beams at him.*

Well! When does this blasphemy start?

BROTHER GEORGE. I think they are a bit late.

BETTY. We are in the right place?

SISTER ANNE. The Anglican Vicar was going to let them do it on the steps of the church!

BETTY. We must all pray for the Church of England. Oh!

ROGER, *a top tabloid reporter, wanders on. He has a camera.*

SISTER ANNE. It's that strange man. Who was hanging around the Baptist hall . . .

BETTY. It's a big boy. From Wapping. No one say anything.

SISTER ANNE. You mean . . . (*Panicking.*) A real reporter? . . .

BETTY. Not a word! I'll do the interviews. He loves me. (*Aside.*) Why has one of the heavies, come down to this little do? On Election Day? (*To the* REPORTER.) Hello Roger! Here I am!

BROTHER GEORGE *looks along the street and goes off.*

ROGER. Hello Betty! Getting your knickers in a twist for the Lord again?

BETTY. Now Roger! I don't want any of that from you!

ROGER. Devil's party myself, Betty.

BETTY. You do the Lord's work without knowing.

BROTHER GEORGE *comes back on, quickly.*

BROTHER GEORGE. They're coming! And it's worse than we thought!

SISTER ANNE. Oh! My tummy's turning.

BETTY (*to the* CONSTABLE). Constable! Do nothing until I make a complaint!

CONSTABLE. Oh, right . . .

BROTHER GEORGE. Let us pray!

SISTER ANNE. Sing!

BROTHER GEORGE. Praise the Lord!

BETTY. We'll go over the street. Hide in that chemist's doorway. Come on!

BROTHER GEORGE. Oh. Isn't that rather . . .

BETTY. What?

BROTHER GEORGE. Sneaky?

ROGER. You've got a seasoned moral campaigner here, old man. Don't teach Saint Betty how to suck eggs.

BETTY. Quite right dear.

As if about to cross a street, through the traffic.

I'm rushing straight to Broadcasting House after this. On call for *News At One*.

ROGER. Messing about in politics Betty?

BETTY. Naughty, naughty! God is politics. Go on everyone! Dodge the traffic . . .

They 'cross the street' and hide. For a moment, the CONSTABLE is alone on the stage, nervous. He takes his radio from his lapel, at the ready.

Off, loud tinny music. A 'Dies Irae'.

Enter a street theatre troupe. A ROMAN CENTURION with a whip. MARY, Christ's Mother. They plant a banner, between sticks, the stick implanted in orange boxes. The banner reads 'PASSION OF A WOMAN VOTER'. They set a tea-chest. On the tea-chest a placard, which reads 'NOBODY CARES. VOTE FOR NOBODY'.

NB: The actors in the passion play have half-face masks. Incongruously, hanging around their necks over their Biblical costumes, they have electric megaphones.

The CENTURION cracks his whip on the pavement.

CONSTABLE (*to himself*): Oi oi!

He begins to mumble into his radio. The taped music goes into a ska beat. The CENTURION and MARY chant, blasting through their megaphones.

MARY. The housewife voter crucified . . .

CENTURION. Jesus Christ, who was she . . .

MARY. Daughter of woman, not of man . . .

CENTURION. She would not vote for man! Man's world! Man's taxes, man's holy Parliament! So crucify the bitch!

The CENTURION cracks the whip on the pavement.

Enter a female CHRIST, dragging a cross. She is wearing a half-mask and is naked but for a traditional Christ loincloth, a housewife's turban and pink fluffy slippers. The pipe of a vacuum cleaner is draped around the cross. Instead of the 'INRI' sign at the top of the cross there is a board, on it the words 'DON'T VOTE'.

MARY (*megaphone*). She shall rent the temple of Parliament! The great seal of men and power shall be cracked! Westminster, She shall throw you down, stone by stone!

As MARY rants, CHRIST and the CENTURION insert the cross in a slot in the top of the tea-chest. CHRIST ascends the cross in the traditional position. The CENTURION cracks the whip on the pavement.

The heads of BROTHER GEORGE and SISTER ANNE poke around the corner of the stage.

SISTER ANNE. Ooh I say!

BROTHER GEORGE. Disgraceful!

CHRIST. Sisters. We will not vote for the man and his works. And today thou shalt be with my Mother in Paradise.

The CENTURION spreads his arms wide. 'John Wayne acting'.

CENTURION (*megaphone*). Truly this was the daughter of God.

ROGER, *camera at the ready*, BETTY *and* SISTER ANNE *and* BROTHER GEORGE *tumble toward the scene. The CONSTABLE's radio crackling.*

All speak at once:

SISTER ANNE. Stop this outrage!

BROTHER GEORGE. Stop that actress's breasts!

ROGER. I gotta get the pix! Betty I want you, with the bint on the cross!

SISTER ANNE. Filth! Cover yourself, cover it up!

ROGER. Jesus! Jesus! Look at me! Poke 'em out Jesus, Jesus!

Then:

BETTY. Oh you sinners, silly-billy people! With your filthy minds, misguided, mocking the faith of decent folk . . .

She is suddenly still. And, at the moment, everyone is still. CHRIST *and* BETTY *are staring at each other.*

The CHRIST *removes her half-mask.*

Judy!

CHRIST/JUDY. Oh Mum, what the fuck are you doing here?

BETTY. Judy!

CENTURION. Fuck. Her Mum has turned up.

MARY. Great, this is great for the play . . .

CENTURION. Oh Gawd! I'll never work again.

SISTER ANNE (*to* BROTHER GEORGE). Her daughter?

ROGER, *photographing at speed.*

ROGER. That was the tip off and this is the story folks!

BETTY. Judy! Get down off that cross at once!

JUDY. St Paul said 'I am crossed out in Christ!'.

BETTY. He said no such thing you stupid girl.

JUDY. Mum! I'm thirty-three years old! As old as he was!

ROGER. Great, oh great!

BETTY. Wicked! I'll get you down off there myself . . .

BROTHER GEORGE. Constable . . .

CONSTABLE. Right, all of you . . .

A scrummage. The actors and the two christians in the mêlée with BETTY *and* JUDY. *The* CONSTABLE *wades in.* ROGER *circles the scene, photographing.*

ROGER. Betty! Betty! What d'ya think of your daughter doing this? Betty!

All speak at once:

CENTURION. Get back, just get back . . .

BETTY. You wicked, wicked . . . God if your father . . . Oh you girl . . .

MARY. Freedom o' speech! What about freedom o' speech!

ROGER. So fucking speak, darling . . .

SISTER ANNE. Sing! Someone, sing a hymn!

Then:

ROGER. Déposition from the cross! 1980's style. Raphael you should'a been living at this hour.

The cross keels over, with all of them falling, in slow motion, into a heap.

Disentangling themselves.

CENTURION. Run!

MARY. Judy come on!

CENTURION. Come on!

MARY. Judy!

CONSTABLE. Not you!

MARY *and* CENTURION *run off. They are heard offstage, shouting 'Judy' . . . 'Judy' . . . But the* CONSTABLE *keeps his hold on* JUDY's *arms.*

SISTER ANNE. Give her something to cover her up.

BROTHER GEORGE. Er, here Miss . . .

He takes off his coat and puts it around JUDY.

SISTER ANNE *stands, helping* BETTY *up. The* CONSTABLE, *one hand on an unresisting* JUDY's *arm, the other at his radio, is sending for help.*

CONSTABLE. Incident at 2 Dog Lane School Polling Station, assistance required, two suspects, going toward West Peckham Estate . . .

The radio crackles.

SISTER ANNE. Oh Mrs Blaze, I am so sorry, we had no idea your daughter . . .

A pause. Embarrassment.

JUDY (*at* BETTY). You make everything dirty. Everything.

BETTY. I? I make dirty?

ROGER. Come on Betty! Interview time.

BETTY. Give me this one Roger. After all the stories I've slipped you. You'll bury this one . . .

JUDY. Listen to her! Listen to her!

The CONSTABLE *pulling* JUDY *away.*

CONSTABLE. Now now.

BETTY. Be fair to me, Roger.

A pause, all looking at ROGER. *Then he backs away.*

ROGER. All right. Don't worry Betty girl. I'll see you all right in the story.

BETTY. Oh! Bless you dear. I'll say a little prayer.

ROGER. That will come in handy.

He is going. He turns.

(*Aside.*) Fifteen years we've printed her muck. She's got it coming to her. If Labour get back in, it'll be no holds barred. But if it's Thatcher again, the paper'll kill the story. The days of right-wing gurus will go on for ever.

He sniffs.

Think I'll go down the Walworth Road. See if I can get a shot o' Kinnock picking his nose. You never know y' luck . . .

He's gone. The sound of a police car's siren. The CONSTABLE *pulling* JUDY *off.*

CONSTABLE. We will want statements from you all.

BETTY. I'll come with you . . .

JUDY *spits on the ground before* BETTY. *Who is frozen.*

The CONSTABLE *and* JUDY *go off.*

SISTER ANNE. The Porn Committee . . . have laid on a tea. At the Baptist Hall. There are cakes, there are buns . . .

BETTY. What I need . . . Need now . . . Is a stiff scotch.

SISTER ANNE. Oh?

BETTY. You go on. I'll have a little prayer.

SISTER ANNE. The Baptist . . .

BETTY, *a flash of violent temper.*

BETTY. I'll find the wretched hall!

SISTER ANNE. But the Police . . .

BETTY. I'll talk to the Police. Just go!

SISTER ANNE *and* BROTHER GEORGE *pause, then turn away, walking off.*

BROTHER GEORGE. Whited sepulchre.

SISTER ANNE. No, surely . . .

BROTHER GEORGE. Feet of clay, there.

SISTER ANNE. I don't think . . .

BROTHER GEORGE. I do.

They are gone. BETTY *alone.*

BETTY. To be a brand . . . Put to the burning. Oh, to catch fire!

She covers her face with her hands. The sound again of a police siren.

She goes off.

Scene Three

5 p.m. South London. Amongst flats.

BRIAN *before us. He has a Harrods plastic bag, much abused. It is full of cans of lager.*

BRIAN. The . . .
fuurst . . .
la la larger . . . ! !

And he holds up a can from the bag, like a magician producing a rabbit from a hat.

First since lunch-time, that is.

A woman's VOICE, *shouting down at him.*

VOICE. Brian! You han't made your bed!

Looking up.

BRIAN. Oh! Dot! Right! (*Aside.*) My sister, Dot. Live with her. Got a wank pit in her spare room.

VOICE. You lazy bugger!

BRIAN. Oh, right! (*Aside.*) Just 'til somthin' turns up. Y'know, while I steady myself.

VOICE. These sheets are disgustin'! You said you'd take 'em down the laundrette.

BRIAN. Give over, Dot! Not in public . . .

VOICE. They're grey! They got beer all over 'em!

BRIAN (*aside*). I mean it's only a poxy council flat. Poxy South London. You'd think it were the fucking Ritz with her.

Hoover, hoover . . . (*Shouts up.*) Can't you take 'em down? I got to see a man in a pub . . .

DOT. You're a lazy, dirty, lazy bugger!

BRIAN. Give us a break, Dot! They open in half an hour. (*Aside.*) I dunno. Days are so short. They just go.

A bundle of two dirty, single sheets is thrown down onto the stage.

DOT. Do your own fuckin' washing. And don't come back 'fore you do!

BRIAN. What do you want to do? Humiliate your own flesh and blood?

DOT. You heard!

Above, a door slammed.

BRIAN. Dunno at all. Survival o' the fittest in't it.

Picking up the sheets, putting them under his arm. He walks off, sheepishly. As . . .

Scene Four

LORD LUDLOW (PAUL) *comes on. He is dressed in evening dress. He is well built, straight-backed. His dress is immaculate. He carries a portable telephone, of the latest design. He is dialling. He stands, legs slightly apart, 'manly', 'suave' in his manner. Harrovian accent.*

PAUL. Meanwhile in another neck of the woods, as they say, a great deal of money is being lost.

Into the telephone.

Jacko, you fucker. Are we or are we not having dinner tonight?

Listens.

'Course I'm not going to the fucking Garrick, last time I dined there I had to sit next to some fucking little High Court Judge. The little cunt threw his custard pudding all over me. No I've booked a table for four at Swanson's.

Listens.

What the fuck do you mean, 'Mustn't gamble' tonight? It's General Election night. The whole fucking country's at the gaming tables. Could lose all, come the dawn find it's a Moscow shade of red. Where would you and I be then? . . . Right. In the hills. Jacko . . .

He pauses. Lowers his voice. MILLY his wife comes on. She is in her early thirties, drawn, withdrawn. She carries a perfect white carnation.

Just a little chemmy. Something light. After a light supper. The Club will stand you half of anything, if you're with me. They like an Earl and his friends at the tables. It encourages the Arabs. Do this for me?

Listens.

Thank you Jacko.

Palms the aerial of the telephone down. Husband and wife look at each other.

A silence.

Then she holds out the carnation. He takes it. He gives her the telephone.

A silence.

Then he begins to try to put the carnation in his button hole.

Children . . . ?

MILLY. Little John rang.

PAUL. Enjoying themselves?

MILLY. His sister was sick.

PAUL. That fool of a husband of your friend Florence. Taking kids on a helicopter trip. I'm not sure I approve.

MILLY. Why do you not approve?

PAUL. It gives them ideas.

MILLY. And what ideas are those?

PAUL. You know. That everything comes easily.

MILLY *scoffs.*

MILLY. Well you should know all about that.

A pause.

PAUL. Milly I don't want to bitch.

MILLY. Am I coming to Swanson's tonight?

PAUL *sighs.*

PAUL. Well are you?

MILLY. I don't want to sit any more, amongst your cronies.

PAUL. No.

Fumbling with the carnation.

Fucking flower . . .

She closes her eyes. A slight sway. Then she opens her eyes. She takes the carnation brushing his hands away. She begins to fix it.

PAUL. Things narrow. You know? Narrow down and I . . . It could all come to pieces, you know. And I've done my best.

He floods with rage. Clenches a fist. Hits it against his side. Then rubs his hand. She stands her ground. They are close together. Then, clumsily, he tries to take her face in his hands to kiss her, but now she flinches away.

He looks at the carnation.

PAUL. Carnation. Death flower.
What will you do? Watch the box?

Nothing from MILLY. He turns and goes.

MILLY *alone, not moving.*

Then she puts the telephone down. Lifts her arms and undoes her hair. She shakes her head, her hair falls.

The telephone rings. She does not answer it.

From the pocket of her skirt, she takes out a large joint of marijuana. She puts it slowly in her mouth, wetting the skin. She takes out a small gold cigarette lighter. She lights the joint. She inhales deeply. She blows the smoke out.

The telephone stops ringing.

MILLY (*aside*). I want to be back in the early seventies, in a secret Chelsea garden. Flowers, by the river, in the sunshine. Drinking wine. Giggling. Feeling naked in a short skirt, my legs long and golden. And a handsome young aristocrat, leaning over me, helplessly in love.

PAUL *comes back on, a strange distortion on his face.*

She instantly steps away.

MILLY. No don't Paul! Oh my God!

He hits her in the stomach.

PAUL. I am in hell . . .

MILLY. Bastard!

PAUL. Don't you see that!

He punches her in a kidney. She doubles and falls.

(*Aside..*) I have forty suits in my dressing room. They are of silk or wool. Identical. They all have the same pattern and cut. Blue, a light stripe.

Clenches his fists.

Life should be so . . . good!

He steps on her head. She yells and rolls.

Looky. It's all right. Don't lie there crying. Looky here.

He takes a fistful of jewels, diamonds, from his pocket.

I went to Cartiers. All the cash I could put together. Thousands worth. Pure, simply cut. So we are all right Milly. If the country goes to the dogs. If the reds take over. If the bastards come for us . . .

He sags, half kneels.

I'll stay in tonight. We'll watch the box. Crack a bottle of the burgundy, we . . .

He pauses, a hand covering his face. Then suddenly he stands.

He holds up a diamond bracelet.

Here. With love.

He throws the bracklet on the floor before her. He goes off, raging. fists clenched.

A silence. MILLY dead still.

Then she moves painfully. She picks up the joint. It is trodden. She picks up the bracelet and dangles it before her face.

In a very faint, high clear voice she sings a few lines from the Eagles' song, 'Desperado'.

MILLY.
'Why don't you come to your senses
You've been out riding fences
　　　　For so long now . . .
These things that are pleasing you
Can hurt you somehow . . .
Oh it's hard to tell
　　　　The night from the day . . .'

She stays on the stage. She hides her head in her arms, bundled up, the telephone before her.

Scene Five

BRIAN *comes on. He carries his Harrods bag and the bundle of dirty sheets. He has an unopened can of lager in his hand.*

BRIAN (*aside*). Where was I? Yeah, that first bite of the first can of a long, long night.

The drinker approaches.

Now some wankers make nothing of this moment. Your scum of the earth, your average boozer, your Millwall supporter, just go rip-bang-wallop.

Whereas your 'artiste', your Leonardo of the lager can . . .

He holds up his left hand, then just its third finger.

God, I'm dying. That taste o' orange peel, with the fizz. No! I got to get some self-discipline. The whole night ahead to get out a' control . . .

He puts the Harrods bag down carefully. He pulls the sheets around his shoulders. He adopts the drinker's stance, legs apart. Holds out the can in his right hand. Finger to the ring.

Here she blows.

Up where the air is fresh 'n' clean.

He pulls the ring. Lager squirts. He sups, wandering off.

Two Labour Party workers come on, BILL, *working class, and* VAL, *middle class. Rosettes, armfuls of pamphlets. Shoulder bags.*

VAL. I wanted to come out earlier.

BILL. Oh yeah?

VAL. But the children. And Hippolyta's in Portugal.

BILL. Hip what?

VAL. Our au pair.

BILL. Gotcha. (*Frowns.*) Hippolyta, isn't that Greek?

VAL. But her boyfriend's Portuguese.

BILL. Ah. Well. That'll be why.

VAL. Why what?

BILL. Why she's in Portugal. (*Aside.*) Help!

VAL. She has her own room. And we give her English lessons. She's free to eat with us . . . And she's got her . . . (*Weakening.*) own key.

BILL. Look, eh, Valerie in't it?

VAL. Val.

BILL. You done this before?

VAL *looks puzzled.*

Canvassing for Labour.

VAL. No, actually. Actually, I'm a bit nervous.

BILL. Don't worry it's a doddle. When did you join the party, Val?

VAL. Last week, in fact. I thought I had to do something.

BILL. Good for you. (*Aside.*) Save me, save me Trotsky!

VAL. What about you?

BILL. Oh . . . I'm Union section. NUT.

VAL. You . . . are a teacher? (*She is scared.*) Not Militant . . .

BILL. Heavy duty workerist tendencies more like, comrade.

VAL. Workerist?

BILL. Roll the Union on etcetera. Look love, shall we get on tryin' to drag Neil Kinnock by his remaining hair, screaming into Number Ten?

VAL. Let's. They say the Labour Party is a broad church.

BILL. Very like a church. Smell a' mothballs and the lead nicked off the roof – right, these call backs. In the flats. These are promises, but the sods haven't turned up at the polls yet. We know from the cards. You clock the system?

VAL. Er . . .

BILL. It's a straightforward knock-up. I'll do numbers one to a hundred, you do a hundred and up . . .

VAL. We're going to split up?

BILL. I'll do a couple o' doors with you. Just say have you voted yet? If they want a babysitter, sit with the baby while they pop round.

VAL. Oh.

BILL. Just get the buggers to vote.

VAL. All right . . .

BILL. Don't worry. These are our people.

BRIAN crosses before them. Carefree, contemplating his third lager can.

BRIAN (*aside*). Can number three. Your first five cans are the lower slopes of Mount Piss-up.

Rips the ring off the can.

VAL. Shall we do him?

BILL. Scraping the barrel a bit.

VAL. Surely he, too, is the great electorate.

She frowns.

But why has he got dirty bedsheets round his neck?

Grins.

Takes all sorts.

BILL. He won't even be on the electoral register . . .

But she is confronting BRIAN.

VAL. 'Scuse me, do you vote?

BRIAN is stunned. He stares at her.

BRIAN. Do I what?

VAL. Will you, tonight?

BRIAN looks puzzled.

VAL. It's only just gone five. You've got until ten. So vote. For the Labour Party.

BRIAN. I got a secret life, you know.

VAL. We've all got our lives, but what about the country? What has Margaret Thatcher ever done for you?

BRIAN. What are you? The Government?

VAL. No, no, we're Labour.

BRIAN. Stuff the Government.

VAL. Labour Party, not the Government. Though we want to be!

BRIAN. Why do you want . . . (*A sweep of an arm.*) To run my life?

VAL. I don't want to run your life . . .

BRIAN. Coming up in the fucking street, trying to run my life . . .

BILL intervenes.

BILL. That's enough, friend.

BRIAN. And who are you, Hitler?

BILL. On your way, friend.

He and BRIAN, eyeball to eyeball.

Have a pamphlet.

He pushes a pamphlet against BRIAN's chest. It flutters to the ground. BRIAN backs away. He lurches up-stage then turns, abusive from a distance.

BRIAN. Gov'ment . . . Police . . . Labour . . . Man on the fucking telly . . . All you, keep off! You don't know me! You don't know my secret life!

BRIAN goes off.

BILL. Don't let it worry you.

She smiles.

VAL. Was that what they call the lumpen proletariat?

BILL. Not the real thing, not at all.

VAL. Oh Lord.

BILL. Tell you what, I'll do the flats. You do Craven Grove. More your thing. I'll still do a couple of doors with you to get you going.

She is angry.

VAL. No. I can handle Craven Grove. Every house costs over a hundred and fifty thousand. Much more my 'kind of thing'.

He looks at her, unsmiling.

BILL. The point of doing this, is to get a Labour Government elected.

VAL. 'Yes, comrade'.

A pause.

BILL. See you back at the committee rooms, then. Oh. No canvassing while EastEnders is on the box. Knock 'em up while Dirty Den is doing his stuff, sure vote loser.

VAL. Right. (*They part. Aside.*) Pig.

BILL (*aside*). God Almighty. We're going to lose.

They go off.

Scene Six

MILLY *still on the stage, huddled before her telephone. She does not look up.*

MILLY. I don't want anything, I'm not ambitious. I just don't want to be who I am.

The telephone rings five times. She does not look at it. It stops ringing.

Not much to want.

At the back, PAUL, 'JACKO' *and two other male friends,* ANDREW *and* HUGH, *come on. 'Street lighting' – blueish, light from polished glass, passing cars.*

JACKO. ⎫   London Nights. Out there . . .

PAUL. ⎬   What did I drive here? The fucking BMW or the fucking Volvo . . .

JACKO. The discos whirr, the roulette tables whirr, the brains of drunks, the wheels of the traffic, whirr whirr, films in the cinema projectors, hamburgers slapped on ten thousand plates, fifteen-year-old girls on high heels, the punters the punted, the muggers and the mugged, the pigeons in Trafalgar Square, whirrrrr!

ANDREW. Pissed again . . .

JACKO. London Nights . . .

PAUL. Fucking keys.

Fumbles in his pockets. Diamonds spill.

HUGH. My God Paul, what's all this? Burglary?

PAUL. S'mine . . .

ANDREW. Loot?

HUGH, *slurred.*

HUGH. Second Earl a' Ludlow, se's a fucking cat burglar!

PAUL. ⎫   You buggers . . .

HUGH. ⎬   Pink Panther! S'a fucking Panther!

JACKO. ⎭   London nights! Diamonds in the gutters, 'long with theatre tickets, spewed up chinese takeaways, old johnnies . . .

ANDREW. Paul what the fuck are you doing?

PAUL. Reds.

ANDREW. What?

They are picking the diamonds up. A WOMAN TRAMP *wanders past.*

PAUL. Stash. Go to the Welsh hills. Small arms.

ANDREW. Pursued by whom?

The TRAMP *has picked up a diamond necklace. She stands, swaying, looking at it.*

TRAMP. You'sha, whatsh a?

ANDREW *relieves the* TRAMP *of it.*

ANDREW. Thank you Jeeves.

The TRAMP, *lurching off.*

TRAMP. You'sha, whatsh a?

HUGH. Come on you drunken farts, let's all go on to Mary Anne's.

PAUL *pocketing the jewels.*

JACKO. What is it Paul? Is it Milly?

PAUL *holding up a car key.*

PAUL. S'all right I'm in the Volvo.

ANDREW. Mary Anne's, one and all . . .

ANDREW *and* HUGH, *peeling away.*

JACKO. Paul!

PAUL *holding* JACKO's *lapels.*

PAUL. Look Jacko will you do this for me? Go on to where . . . there you're going. I'll be with you. Say I'm with you.

JACKO. Brigade spirit?

PAUL. I'm fucking with you all the time right?

JACKO. My dear fellow, don't . . .

PAUL. With you. With you.

He runs off.

JACKO. Paul!

ANDREW. Where is the drunken Earl?

JACKO. A piss up a dark alley. He's with us. On we go.

HUGH. What's the time?

ANDREW. Twelve o' twelve-thirty.

HUGH. Fuck and damnation!

ANDREW. What?

HUGH. I forgot to vote.

They are going off.

ANDREW. What do you want to fucking vote for?

HUGH. Well I'm the only one of you who who can. You buggers are all in the House of Lords.

JACKO. Never pissed on those portals myself.

Point of principle . . .

They are gone.

MILLY.
If I were not me, what would I . . .
. . . wear?

What would I know? What would I think?

What would be the colour of my hair?

How would I . . .

Move? Smile? Turn . . .

Where would I live?

Who . . .

would I love?

At the back of the dark stage, a spotlight, very bright, switches on then at once, dies. In it a figure of a WOMAN, in a strange, long dress, barefoot, with MILLY's long blonde hair. The figure is turning on the ball of a bare foot, a shrugging gesture, which may mean 'hello', or may be dismissive – 'hard luck'.

The figure gone. MILLY starts and glances over her shoulder. She shivers. She remains on the stage.

Scene Seven

MILLY, *on the stage huddled before the telephone.*

JUDY *comes on. She carries a pair of garden shears. Her arms are full of cut and mutilated flowers. She strews the flowers about the floor, lethargic gestures. She stands, looking out, the shears dangling from her hand.*
BETTY *comes on. She stops.*

BETTY. Judy. Thank God you got back home, dear.

Nothing from JUDY. BETTY gushes.

Oh I'm dead on my feet. First the BBC wanted me on *Newsnight Special*, then they didn't. Was I furious! I made a scene they won't forget. And thank the good Lord, it looks like Mrs Thatcher is back in.

It's wonderful to think that God is working his purpose out, through an English Prime Minister.

She realises. She lifts her glasses and looks around the floor.

JUDY *lets the shears fall from her hand. They clatter on the stage.*

What have you done? The garden.

She pauses. Then she rushes off. She comes back onto the back of the stage, as if out to a garden. She has a flashlight. She flits it about her in bewilderment.

JUDY (*aside*). Why do I hate her so? Because everything I do, is what she does. She is a fundamentalist, I am a fundamentalist. She to one extreme, I to another. I can only be what she is, the other way round. I know the way she thinks, I feel it in my own thoughts. I hear the edge of her voice in my voice. When I am her age, I know my body will be just like hers.

BETTY *at the back, rushing about, 'in the garden'.*

BETTY. How could you . . . how could you!

She stops. The flashlight on a particular spot.

Oh look. My lilies too. Little madam! Give her a good thwack on the backside! Her father . . .

But her father is in America. With a harlot from Chicago . . .

Oh please!

Flitting the flashlight 'around the garden'.

Don't tell the media that! So many humiliations. I know I am, to many, a laughing-stock. But that about Hugh, I could not bear . . .

Someone there? *Express, Sun, Star?* They don't throw Christians to the lions now, they throw them to mockery. Which is worse?

No!

Closes her eyes.

Is a wrecked garden in Wimbledon to be my Gethsemane?

She trembles, mouth open. Wet lower lip.

When I was a little girl, nine years old, I read John Bunyan's *Pilgrim's Progress*. Under the bedclothes, at night, with a torch. There were fearsome pictures. The Slough of Despond. The Castle of Giant Despair. I wanted to scream.

Oh Lord, this world is a terrible place.

She composes herself. She goes back 'into the kitchen'.

Well you ungrateful little madam . . .

JUDY. Don't start Mum . . .

BETTY. Arrested, naked in the street for all to see! And what are the police going to do?

JUDY. No charges. You know there'll be no charges! You rang the station! And got me out, because of who you are!

BETTY. For which I get no thanks?

They glare at each other.

A pause.

Look at the state of your life . . .

JUDY. I was chucked out of my flat, that's all . . .

BETTY. No money, thirty-three, having to come begging to me for a roof over your head . . .

JUDY. You said you'd love me at home . . .

BETTY. But you've been here six months! Sleeping 'til midday, out to heaven knows when. You would think, with all I do for people, the Lord would give me a daughter . . . but no.

JUDY. Mother, has it never struck you that we both want the same thing?

BETTY. Never!

JUDY. You and your Christian lunatics, your anti-porners, your clean-up TV campaigners, in your gospel halls? I and my friends, street-theatre clowns, squatters, in our resource centres in shabby shops? We all want a new world. That has . . . Light. That's human, and decent, and . . . Clean?

We both want . . . A new Jerusalem?

BETTY. Clean? You say the word 'clean'? Wash your mouth out, girl. What was that thing I found in your room?

JUDY. Thing?

BETTY. On top of the wardrobe!

JUDY. You've searched my room?

BETTY. That wicked, filthy thing!

JUDY. You mean my vibrator?

She smirks.

Try it Mum. Next time you feel a prayer coming on.

From BETTY *a deep sound.*

BETTY. Ooooh, ooooh.

JUDY. We must . . . Oh I hate talking like this . . . Mum, we must find out real selves.

BETTY. We must find God.

JUDY. Have you seen how people are living out there? On the estates? Their only chance is to save themselves.

BETTY. Salvation is Heaven's gift. It is certainly not the gift of a Lesbian theatre company performing in the nude. 'Find your real self?' Will you do that with some battery operated, plastic carrot, that you stick up your private parts?

JUDY. Sometimes I think it's you that's got the dirty mind.

BETTY. Nothing shocks me, girl. When you campaign against immorality, you learn the worst.

None of it shocks me.

A pause.

It just makes me fall to my knees and pray.

JUDY. I'm not going to kneel down and close my eyes with you Mum. I've done that so often, just not to have this argument . . .

BETTY. Just a little one.

JUDY. No.

BETTY. A quick word with Him . . .

JUDY. No!

BETTY. 'Jerusalem' . . . Ooooh . . . I can see your 'holy city' my girl. The city of perpetual indulgence. Your only church a

VD clinic. Abuse of the body, slavery to all that's base.

JUDY. I can see your 'Jerusalem'. A police state. All human desires, censored. 'Hallelujahs' broadcast on megaphones at each street corner. And lovers torn apart by cops at night.

A pause. They look at each other, appalled.

BETTY. Don't have anything more to do with those people, Judy. Those . . . 'women'. Please.

JUDY. Do you want to meet my lover? She is very sweet. You'd like her.

BETTY. Ooooh. I . . .

JUDY. Mum.

BETTY. Don't touch me!

They are looking at each other. BETTY, *mouth open, wet lower lip. Then she rushes off.*

JUDY (*aside*). Just one crack. In the lines of a famous face. Just one glimpse that you may be wrong, Mum.

JUDY *looks about her. She picks up the garden shears. She opens and shuts them a couple of times, despondently.*

Well come on, you stupid cow. Come back and tell me Jesus forgives. We'll have a cup of cocoa, then I'll kneel down with you in tears. For a bit of peace and quiet. I . . .

The sound of a car starting.

Mum? Mum?

Car lights pass across the back wall of the stage.

Mum!

JUDY *rushes off and back on at the back of the stage.*

Where's she gone? (*Aside.*) How strong is she? Not that much, after all?

A look of horror, very like BETTY's *wet lip look.*

I should know. I do know. Oh God, what have I done?

She rushes off.

The stage remains strewn with flowers until the end of the act.

Scene Eight

MILLY *alone. The stage now littered with flowers.*

PAUL *lurches on. She looks up at him sharply.*

PAUL. Shorry.

MILLY. What did you say, what did you say to me?

A silence.

PAUL. Sorry, slipped up.

MILLY (*aside*). You look at the eyes for the tell-tale sign. The muscles in his cheeks, gone slack. The sign that he is over the edge.

PAUL. Fair's fair.

MILLY (*aside*). I married an Earl. 'My elevation' said my friends, bitchily. My ascension into the clouds.

PAUL. The bracelet. It was thirty thousand. Give it back to me.

MILLY. Oh. (*Laughs.*) Do you mean this?

She dangles the bracelet before him.

PAUL. Rush of blood to the head. (*Both still.*) I'll leave you alone. I'll go. Loosh myself!

(*He hiccups.*) In the hills.

MILLY. Ha!

She swallows the bracelet. They look at each other, shocked.

MILLY, *oddly matter-of-fact.*

I swallowed it.

She begins to giggle.

PAUL. That's my life! Milly, Milly . . . Godsake, get to the bathroom . . . spoon, tongue . . . Get it out. God! What? Mustard, hot water . . .

Her giggles are uncontrollable.

Here!

He grabs her. She pummels him with her fists and squirms away, laughing.

MILLY. What you going to do? Wait down the loo pan? Hey? Where is my Lord? My Lord is down my loo . . .

PAUL (*aside*). I always eat the same thing. First course, scotch smoked salmon.

Second, lamb cutlets, hot in winter, in summer, jellied. Then strawberry ice-cream.

The best meal in the world. Again and again . . .

Fist clenched, into a rage.

Again! And again! And again!

He grabs MILLY *by the hair. She grabs his legs.*

Again! Again! Again! Again!

He stops. Lovingly.

Oh Milly, Milly, let me pat you on the back. Give you a rub? Let's go and make love . . . You must cough it up. You . . .

She is hit by a pain.

MILLY. Oh! You'll . . . Have . . to split me open. Split me, you bastard.

Bad pain.

Oh!

She looks up startled. She cannot speak. She has a spasm. They look at each other. She puts a hand out to him.

PAUL. Worth it. Ha! Thirty grand!

She tries to speak.

Cheap at the price! My freedom!

She tries to move toward him. He takes a step away, then runs off, weeping.

MILLY, *her hands to her mouth, has a convulsion. Then she is still. She takes her hands away from her mouth. She has got the bracelet up. She stares at it. She begins to laugh.*

The telephone rings. She lifts it at once.

MILLY. Oh Geoffrey my darling, the bastard . . .

She begins to laugh.

No I'm fine, fine. I'm coming round to you, now. Now.

She holds the bracelet up, looking at it. Then goes off quickly.

Scene Nine

MILLY *on the stage.*

Elsewhere, South London. Outside a town hall.

Off, raucous singing of 'For he's a jolly good fellow'.

Bill *comes on.*

BILL (*aside*). Defeat. Rage. Strategy. I am knackered.

VAL *comes on.*

VAL. All those Tory hooray Henrys, celebrating. The flesh crawls.

She bumps into BILL.

Oh hello.

He does not recognize her.

Remember me? We canvassed. See years ago . . .

BILL. Oh yeah. Valerie in't it?

VAL. Val . . .

BILL. Come for the town hall wake?

VAL. They said there was a recount. On Election Special. I mean, the people I'm with were getting maudlin. And most of them are Alliance anyway. So I thought I'd come down here . . .

BILL. Right.

VAL: Is there any hope?

BILL. We've lost.

VAL. How do you know?

BILL. The inside word is a hundred and fifty-two votes.

VAL. Why bother with a recount then?

BILL *shrugs.*

BILL. Be bloody minded. Keep the bastards up all night.

VAL. But round here was Labour for years. I mean – the state of the flats . . . Why did we lose? The candidate?

BILL, *blank.*

BILL. How do you mean?

VAL. L . . . Loony left? I mean, she was on the Liberal Party hit list . . .

BILL *scoffs*.

Two other party workers come on, DON *and* JEFF. *They carry a sagging banner.* DON *has a big bunch of red roses, which are the worse for wear.*

VAL, *voice trailing out . . .*

VAL. And didn't she go to see the Sinn Feiners, with Ken Livingstone . . .

DON. Roses! Roses! I am sick of roses!

Throws them down and kicks them about.

JEFF. A hundred and fifty-two votes, a hundred and fifty-two stinking, stupid lazy bums, who couldn't get off the settee away from the box, down to vote.

DON: I don't want to wave a rose like a wally. I want a red flag.

VAL *is determined to join in.*

VAL. Yes, but I think people quite liked the Kinnock rose. President Mitterand's got one . . .

JEFF. And what have they got? A pig Tory, thirty-eight, chin of pink sausages over 'is collar, all after-shave and pissed in the Turf Club . . . You fucking idiots, that what you want?

VAL. I don't think we should blame the electors.

They all stare at her.

I mean this is a democracy.

JEFF. Yeah. A democracy of fools.

A pause.

DON. Coming on to rain. Better roll the banner up. Don't want it to shrink . . .

Begins to do so.

JEFF. Right!

Claps hands.

Who's for the All Night Victory Barbecue?

DON. What Victory?

JEFF. All right, the All Night Defeat Barbecue. We better get over there. The Party bought fifty double litres of Rioja, not to mention fifteen sacks o' chicken drumsticks . . .

DON. Have to have it under umbrellas. With this rain.

JEFF. Joan over there already?

BILL. Dunno.

DON. Well, where is she?

JEFF. Yeah, where is our comrade Candidate? At this our darkest hour . . .

DON. That speech was bloody odd. With a recount going on.

JEFF. Should be here with the walking wounded.

They are looking at BILL.

Bill?

BILL. I know where to find her.

DON. Then do so, Comrade.

BILL. Go to the barbecue. I'll bring her.

He walks off, one hand in a pocket, the other closing his lapels to his throat.

DON. Oi, oi!

JEFF. Really?

DON. Very much so.

VAL. 'Scuse me . . .

They ignore VAL.

JEFF. Since when?

DON. Last party conference but one. When Neil purged the Militants.

JEFF. And our local Robespierre purged our Candidate's knickers?

DON. Now, now . . .

VAL. 'Scuse me but can I join in?

They look at her.

Can I come to the barbecue?

JEFF. You in the Party?

VAL. Yes, I joined to do some canvassing.

DON. And how was it?

VAL. It . . .

A pause.

Was one of the most horrible experiences of my life.

JEFF. Comrade!

DON. One for all and all for a plastic cup o' Spanish plonk!

JEFF. Or ten.

DON. One for all . . .

They enclose arms around either side of VAL.

JEFF. For one.

DON. Close the ranks. We're all terrorists now.

Heavy rain. They flinch.

Fucking rain. We can't move the barbecue indoors. We'd burn the scout hall down . . .

They scuttle off.

Scene Ten

On Southwark Bridge. Night.

JOAN. *She is well dressed, an elegant raincoat. She wears a large Labour Party rosette. Her hair is wet. She looks 'down into the water'.*

BILL *runs on. He sees her at a distance and stops.*

BILL. Bridge over the Thames. Before the City of London, the fortress, the banks.

A forgotten bridge at night.

He approaches JOAN.

JOAN. Ah yes, Bill.

BILL. Does the candidate weep?

JOAN. Not at all. We nearly won.

BILL. Why did you disappear?

JOAN. Work on my speech. For the Victory Party. Is the barbecue . . ?

BILL. Well underway. It's horribly late, Joanie . . .

JOAN. It'll go on for hours. Sausages and red wine for breakfast.

BILL. Looks like it.

JOAN. Neil sent a message. He said he was very pleased, very proud.

BILL. What would he have said if we'd won? That he was sick as a parrot?

JOAN. Deeee . . .

BILL ⎫
JOAN ⎬   Featism.

BILL. OK. OK.

She grins, standing confidently before him.

Are you all right?

JOAN. What did the *Daily Express* call me? Tough cookie?

BILL. Labour Left's Boadicea?

JOAN. Left loony harpy . . .

BILL. That was *The Sun*.

She laughs. They look at each other.

JOAN. You go and keep them sweet, love. Keep the barby going under umbrellas, if needs must. Cooking in bad weather, that's what we're in for, the next five years. Socialists lighting their fires, in the hard rain?

BILL. That the speech?

JOAN. Something like.

She shrugs.

I know, I know, but they'll all be pissed.

BILL. Sure you don't want me to hang about?

JOAN. No. My car's at the end of the bridge.

BILL. Fine.

A pause. He goes to her, they embrace and kiss. He steps back.

Half an hour. No more.

He hesitates, then turns away.

JOAN: Bill?

He turns back.

Do you have a crystal clear idea of what a just, democractic, socialist England would be like? A communist England?

BILL. Hey now . . .

JOAN. No! Really like. To breathe in. Go through a door. Get on a bus, if buses there will be. Do you have any idea?

BILL. No. 'Course I don't.

JOAN. Nor do I.

BILL. Babbling of Utopia?

JOAN. Yes. I am.

BILL. A communist society would be made by its citizens. It would be up to them if they had buses. Or doors, come to that.

JOAN. So by definition Utopia cannot be described?

BILL. Did Marx?

JOAN. William Morris tried.

BILL. Oh yeah. Endless country dancing, with the sun out all the time.

JOAN. People want to know what we want, Bill. On the doorstep. And we can't describe it. Only flat, lead phrases . . . Dignity of working people . . . Right to work . . . Healthcare, pensions, decent life . . . blah, blah. I mean what, what life?

BILL. I don't know why you're talking like this. You know all the answers.

JOAN. Yes. I do. It is pointless talking of Utopia. What matters is the here and now. Concrete struggle. On the concrete.

BILL. Strategy. The gains, the losses.

JOAN. Gains, losses.

BILL. The real world.

JOAN. Oh yes. The dear, cracked concrete . . . the real world. Which we love so much. I am just so angry!

BILL. 'Better a long, cold anger . . .

JOAN. . . . Than a brief fire.'

BILL. Well. (*He shrugs.*) There you go.

JOAN. Yes.

BILL. Ide . . . ol . . . ogy.

JOAN. Ideology. Don't worry, the candidate has the line. Hard and secure. Go down to Brighton tomorrow, shall we?

BILL. Oh yeah! Let us do that.

JOAN. Look at the sea.

BILL. Fish supper?

JOAN. Book into the Ship Hotel? A night, double-room, shower?

BILL. You bet your arse, mate.

JOAN. I will, I do.

A pause.

Twenty minutes, Bill.

He nods. He turns away.

BILL (*aside*). We made love, the first time, on this bridge. Night like this too, rain. Under the walls of the City of London. The castles of money. Leant against the parapet, standing up! She didn't give it a moment's thought, though I was scared sick. Eyes over her shoulder, the while. A panda car coming along? 'Primary school teacher bonks Labour Candidate on a London Bridge?' Who says there's no romance on the Left?

He goes off.

JOAN (*aside*). Upon the candidate let all the sins . . .

She scoffs. A pause.

They're all at it back there. Heating their arguments in bad wine in polystyrene cups. The post-mortem, the old rows. The left shouting 'not enough socialism', the right shouting 'too much'. The centre – Cheshire cats, grinning, relieved the party lost, 'cos now they can really sort out people . . . like . . . me.

And a wind will come . . . Whirl us all up, into the trees. Committees in their birds nests. Tree sways. Wind and rain. Red rags, twigs.

She stamps her foot. Stamps again and whirls, once.

All blown away. God I need a fag. No, you don't. You gave up, for the campaign.

She waits a second.

Yes, you do.

She takes out cigarettes and matches, lights up and sucks blissfully.

An empty beer can flies onto the stage.

And BRIAN comes on. He still has his Harrods bag and bedsheets. He is very drunk. He is having a football fantasy.

BRIAN. N' a long cross, deep from deep mid-field! And the striker! Runs thirty fuckin' yards! Into the box! And with his noddle, bang!

BRIAN makes a lurching attempt at a few yards run, a jump, a header. He falls over. He is crying. He wipes his eye with a corner of the bed sheets.

Split second. So fuckin' beautiful. What I'd give for that.

He staggers to his feet and goes off sadly, head bowed. He and JOAN have not seen each other.

JOAN *blows more smoke.*

JOAN. The angels . . . (*She looks into the smoke.*) cannot tell the living from the dead. (*She shivers.*)

No, not religion! I can't go that way! The fate of burnt-out comrades . . . Old communist poets, kneeling before the Pope . . . Angels?

If there are angels, they are . . . (*She pauses.*) Us?

BRIAN *strides back onto the stage making a cricket batsman's forward drive, a mighty six. His Harrods bag swings from his wrist and pulls him round.*

A bloom of light. A batsman in full whites, white helmet, executing the stroke expertly. The light dies.

BRIAN. Out o' the ground!

JOAN *turns. They stare at each other.*

(*To himself.*) Oooh. Legs.

He wipes his nose on his sleeve. Staggers a side step.

Hello shweeheart!

JOAN (*to herself*). Mm. Now is *that* angelic? Sometimes it's a fucking drag, to believe we are all born good . . .

BRIAN. Tight little bum under there, I can tell. La mumba bumba!

He makes a grotesque wiggle of his backside. As, for a few seconds, a shaft of red light blooms. In it a young woman in a WHORE's outfit – black corset, black stockings, suspenders, high heels, red carnation in her hair. She moves her hips and knees, as if mocking BRIAN's movement. The light dies.

BRIAN, *approaching JOAN.*

Come fly with me?

JOAN. Where do you want to be kicked? Front teeth or balls?

BRIAN. Hunh? Don't y' fink I can fly?

JOAN, *to herself. Looking away.*

JOAN. Oh London. All your sons.

BRIAN *hefts himself, with difficulty, up 'on the parapet'. That is, he squirms on then stands gingerly and walks along the very edge of the stage.*

JOAN. What are you doing?

BRIAN. Here I do, I can!

JOAN (*aside*). Oh no. Another waif and stray. (*At* BRIAN.) Get down! You'll fall in the river.

BRIAN, *terrible singing of a line from 10cc.*

BRIAN. 'Too many broken hearts have fallen in the river.'

JOAN, *fast, a line in her head from the same song.*

JOAN. 'Communication is the problem to the answer.' (*At* BRIAN.) You'll fall! You know, 'Drown?' 'Glug glug?'

BRIAN. I'm gonna fly! Ferra second! It'll . . . Be boo. . .tiful.

He looks at her in horror.

I can't move.

JOAN. Tough shit.

BRIAN. Help me.

JOAN. Join the Labour Party?

BRIAN. Yeah! Anythin'! Get me down!

JOAN (*aside*). Ah well! Organisation. That's what the people need.

She hitches up her raincoat and skirt and climbs up 'on the parapet', nimbly. She faces BRIAN. She holds out her hands.

JOAN. Just take my hands and we'll jump. That way.

Lightly.

Not that way.

A silence.

BRIAN. No.

JOAN. Take my hands. Jump down.

BRIAN. I got a secret life . . .

JOAN. Here.

*She takes his hands. He pulls back. They
lose balance. They fall from the bridge into
the river. That is: they teeter on the edge of
the stage, fighting for balance. A rushing
sound, air and blood in the ears. They snap
rigid, both arms up. Light, deep blue and
green.*

BRIAN. Glug.

JOAN. Glug.

*A blinding flash of white light illuminating
the entire stage.*

BRIAN *and* JOAN *their heads right back,
mouths wide.*

Blackout. And . . .

Scene Eleven

PAUL *is there, in a patch of 'street lighting'.
He is hunched holding his belly.*

PAUL (*aside*). Born noble. To be put to the
test.

But the times are mean.

Oh to live in apocalyptic times. A war. So a
man can put up a good show!

But not bloody likely, in the England of the
eighties. The dog days of little shopkeepers.
No red revolution, no chaps from the old
regiment in North Wales.

What test then, in these times, for the high
born desperado? Build up mighty gambling
debts. Choke a wife . . . Life out of her . . .

Hides his face.

Elsewhere on the stage, JUDY.

JUDY (*aside*). Someone you love runs out of
the front door in London. What do you do,
where do you go?

The Mall? She loved royal occasions.
Tower Hill? She used to preach there, with
the loonies, before the media took her up . . .

Come back Mummy, you bitch. I don't
want you to go away. I want to hate and
scream at you!

A pause.

I'm afraid.

The light around JUDY *dies.* PAUL *again,
to the edge of the stage.*

PAUL. To throw oneself into a test. A swim.

The Hellespont.

Chuck yourself away, to fate.

PAUL *looks down. Light elsewhere on*
BETTY, *who is on her knees. Near her a
broken, rusted child's pushchair. Light off
the water. She is under Vauxhall Bridge at
low tide.*

BETTY. Down. Under the bridge. River of
faith. Dear God this is a dreadful place, at
the heart of the world.

A pause, mouth open, listening.

Yes Lord, my life Lord.

She crawls forward.

A walk on the filthy water.

*The brilliant flash of white light that
illuminates the entire stage. At the back*
JUDY *and* MILLY, *the telephone to her
face, are revealed.*

BETTY *kneeling, hands snapped up above
her head.* PAUL, *standing on the edge of
the stage. The blue and green 'drowning
light'.*

ACT TWO

1. SUMMER.

A green and red stage.

Scene One

Seven hundred years from then. A dawn.

BRIAN *lies unconcious, soaked. Marshland. He is face up. It rains.*

A man and a woman, DRAW *and* A'BET, *watch him. They are swathed in oilskin cloaks.* DRAW *holds a large, asymmetrical umbrella above them.*

DRAW. Do y' get anything?

A'BET. Oh he's in luck. And alive.

A pause.

DRAW. He doesn't? No.

A'BET. No.

DRAW. All night, y'reckon? In this weather? Out in the marshes?

They wait, listening.

A'BET. That's what he says.

DRAW. A man in trouble. Tasty.

A'BET. Hunh hunh.

They move towards BRIAN. A'BET *starts.*

A'BET. Oh.

DRAW. What?

A'BET. He's a boozer.

DRAW. How d'you know that?

A'BET. I know. I was.

DRAW. To see what it was like?

A'BET ⎫
DRAW ⎭ And what was it . . .

A'BET. Flashes o' yellow. Orange. Black. Y' head a red pimple.

DRAW. Like that!

He laughs. They approach. A'BET *bends and, as if with an osteopath's hold, lifts* BRIAN. *A hand on his side.*

A'BET. Bad lungs.

DRAW *stifles a cry. He and* A'BET *stare at each other, at a loss.*

A moment.

DRAW. He's dying.

A'BET. No one dies like that.

DRAW. He must be.

They look at each other, at a loss.

Leave him?

A'BET. His heart's strong, though. Liver's swollen though, but nothing good food, good nights won't right.

DRAW. But what was that out of him, just then?

A'BET. He's violent.

DRAW. Good reason to leave him alone. He'll be flying, through something personal . . .

A'BET. I don't think this one knows how t'do that.

A pause.

We'll get him into the boat, and back to the house. And advice.

DRAW, *in sudden agreement.*

DRAW. Yes, we're right.

DRAW *swirls his cloak and gathers* BRIAN *up, over his shoulder. Their apprehensive mood is quite gone.*

So! When were you a boozer?

A'BET. Oh, in my teens.

DRAW. Beer, wine?

A'BET. Wine, wine. I wanted to be an artist. On walls.

They are walking away.

DRAW. Graffitti? Figures?

A'BET. Sort a' . . .

A gesture.

swirls. Wine made the swirls more . . .

DRAW. Swirly?

A'BET. Swirly.

DRAW. Why did you stop?

A'BET ⎫
DRAW ⎭ Ran out of walls.

They stop and look at each other.

A'BET
DRAW } Ran out of wine.

They laugh and go off.

Scene Two

JOAN *shivering. Bedraggled. She looks at her hands. She holds her head. She peers forward from between her fingers.*

JOAN. Water? Little . . .

She frowns.

Islands?

Covers her eyes.

Shaking! Stop!

She controls herself. She looks again.

There is water. There are islands. Paths. Footbridges. Are there buildings there or not?

She controls a wave of panic and tries again.

Smoke. What, chimneys? Beyond the trees. Nothing's near, no, everything's near.

She holds out her hands, looks at them, turns them over, then stuffs them in her mouth with panic. She speaks through her fingers.

It is not fair. For a paid-up atheist to fall into the river. And wake up to find there is life after death!

No. I'm ill. Get to casualty. St. Thomas's.

She looks about, waves.

Taxi!

Off a whirring sound that rises and falls like a child's whizzer toy. She scuttles away.

JACE, *a jeweller, comes on. He carries a small lathe. It is shining, metallic, inexplicable. It is on a tray around his neck, the strap is multi-coloured, glittering with stones that catch the light. He has a large, irregularly shaped bag slung across his shoulder, it is elaborate, straps, many small pockets. He has a cape, its hem is studded with coloured stones.*

He squats. He sets up his lathe. The tray has little legs which unfold, to make a low table.

JACE (*to himself*). Damp, when you get the damp air. Condensation. Mol – ec – u – lar. That be. That.

As if someone has said something.

What?

Ai! Talk to m'sel. I do, I do, not a thinker. All in things. Who do need thought?

Nowt but in things.

He touches the lathe. It whirrs – the 'whizzer' sound. He takes a small cylinder of heavy metal from a pocket of his bag. He puts the metal cylinder into the lathe. He concentrates.

Tricky, tricky.

He shifts on his haunches and puts his hand on the lathe.

Shining. Perfect in zeal.

The noise of the lathe rises to a high pitch. JOAN dashes from her hiding place.

JACE *loses concentration and cuts his hand. He yells. The lathe dies down. He holds his wrist. Blood.*

Oh no, hand! What you doin'? Hand, oh!

JACE *and* JOAN *stare at each other.*

Y' help me here.

JOAN. What?

JACE *holds out his hand.*

JACE. Bandanna.

JOAN. I don't . . .

JACE. Inna bag!

JOAN. Oh, yes.

She goes to his bag.

What am I looking for?

JACE. Blue! Blue bandana!

She takes a blue, square cloth from his bag.

She looks at it. Sniffs it. He is holding out his injured hand, trustingly.

JOAN. How do I do this?

JACE *in pain, bewildered.*

JACE. Whatever way you do.

JOAN. Er . . .

She folds the square into a triangle. She wraps it around his injured hand. He looks at her quizzically.

JACE. Y' from the Americas, then?

JOAN. America? No.

JACE. Are y' sick? You are, y're shrammed cold. Little bottom pocket of the bag, go on, take one.

She does so and takes out what looks like an old-fashioned sweet, in a twist of paper.

JOAN. Sweets?

JACE. Y' what?

JOAN. What are these, Fisherman's Friends?

JACE. Y' what?

She puts 'the sweet' into her mouth.

That'll warm y'.

She retches and spits it out.

That don't warm y'?

JOAN. Water . . .

JACE *takes out a jug from his bag, takes a cork out and hands the jug to her. She drinks.*

JOAN. Have you got the whole world in there?

JACE. Right. All my world. M'sel, in that bag.

JOAN. Why did you think I'm from the States?

JACE. All from states, in't we? Health, mind . . .

JOAN. No . . . Why did you think I'm from America?

JACE. No offence. Y'smell strange that's all. Y' stink.

Very interested.

What that come from, what you eat?

JOAN. Look, I'm from London. Here.

JACE. The Thames Valley?

JOAN. London.

JACE. Yup, there're so many names. For places. N' people. Names like weeds, cropping up all over. One of my kids, so many love the blighter he's got about thirty names on him. To me he's Hoppy, though. Always will be. That was my name, when he was born. His Mum took it from me for him. You're still shrammed, here.

He lifts his cloak. She hesitates, then snuggles beneath it. He puts his arm around her.

If you're lost, don't think I can find you for you. Sorry. Your bad luck hitting me. I not got much up top.

JOAN (*aside*). Arrive in Heaven? To be picked up by a thick angel?

JACE. And I can't work now, by the look of it.

He holds out his hand.

JOAN. What . . . work do you do?

JACE. Jeweller, in't I.

He takes out a stone and shows it to her.

JOAN. That's so beautiful.

JACE. Here you are then.

He gives it to her.

JOAN. How much?

JACE. How much? Well I haven't got many of 'em, that's half a year's work there. But I got another five stashed away.

JACE. No, what do you want for it? I mean, you want me to buy this?

JACE looks puzzled.

JOAN. You want me to have this? A gift?

JACE. You don't *have* it do you? A jewel. A jewel belongs to itself. All you can do is carry it around. Lose it. Pass it on. Chuck it away.

JACE. But . . . What's it worth?

JACE. To me? My life of course. What's it worth to you?

JOAN stares at the palm of her hand.

JOAN. I don't know, I don't know.

JACE. Seeing I've bust m'hand, d'you want to take over?

JOAN is lost.

The jewellery. I'll teach you.

JOAN (*aside*). An entrepreneur, in Paradise?

JACE. Come on, there's a house I use. There'll be people having breakfast.

They stand, their arms around each other under the cape.

JOAN. Where is this house?

JACE. By Southwark Bridge.

JOAN. Southwark Bridge?

A pause.

(*Aside*). The future. It's . . . crowded.

Scene Three

PAUL *sneaks onto the stage. He carries a thick stick, as a club.*

PAUL (*aside*). Why do other people . . . always have to be there? With their boring, stupid little lives?

Packed into a room when you open a door. Breathing on you in their thousands when you walk down a street.

Give me . . . Desert Island Discs. One book of my choice? Good hard Swedish porn. One object of my choice? A grand piano at concert pitch. A Steinway in the jungle. I'll teach myself to play, plink plonk, year after year. J.S. Bach, 'The Well Tempered Clavier', dawn to dusk, on a coral beach, against the sound of the sea in an empty world.

I'd be happy.

A 'Greenlander' comes on at the back, looking about, cautiously. Her name is SIU. *She wears a large brown leather cape, head and face hidden by a hood. The cape swirls with a hiss over the stage as she turns this way then that.*

That weirdo again. It's been following me for hours, whatever it is. Some kind of bloody hippy.

(*To* SIU) All right you.

NB: SIU *is played by the actress who played* MILLY *in Act One, but at first a man's voice comes from the figure – a trick, an actor in the wings speaking the lines.*

SIU *turns toward* PAUL *and is still.* PAUL *brandishes the club.*

I warn you, you freak! I have a fucking mean golf swing. So bugger off.

SIU (*voice-off*). Sorry, love. I not been well . . .

SIU (*on-stage*). . . . . Very down. Very sick, actually . . .

SIU (*off-stage*). . . . . Still am.

A pause. PAUL *looks off-stage. Then back at* SIU *on-stage when she speaks.*

SIU (*on-stage*). . . . . Some days are better than others. I think it's lifted. Then it comes back. Usually round this time a' day . . .

SIU (*off-stage*). . . . . It grips me . . .

SIU (*on-stage*). . . . . It gets me very bad.

PAUL. Sick?

SIU (*on-stage*). I don't want to put to any trouble . . .

SIU *takes a step toward* PAUL.

PAUL. Stay there!

SIU (*on-stage*). I don't want to bother you at all, really, I don't. Not with what I've got . . .

PAUL (*aside*). Fucking Ada. (*To* SIU.) Just stay there!

A pause. Both still.

SIU (*on-stage*). Oh! (Laughs.) No, you can't catch it . . . (SIU *off-stage, laughing.*)

SIU (*off-stage*). What a queer idea you got about disease!

PAUL *about to speak.*

SIU (*on-stage*). You're safe, really!

SIU (*off-stage*). Funny. Each age has got its own diseases. Hundreds of years on, you've got a whole new choice o' what to die from.

SIU (*on-stage*). Though die you do, don't you.

The masked SIU *on-stage, a graceful shrug, hands out, palms exposed.*

PAUL *stares. Then he spins. He looks off-stage again, then at* SIU *on-stage.*

The danger is I'll catch something from you.

Falters.

It's a mental illness. You, I think . . . have got it too.

A wheel with numbers, it's spinning in your head. Green tables. Low lights. You go deep . . . You're drowning, in a little glass in your hand.

You . . . 'gamble'?

Your name's Paul.

PAUL. What are you? Some kind of mind reader? Some two-bit ventriloquist? Some cheapo kind of fucking Variety act?

SIU (*off-stage*). Vent?

SIU (*on-stage*). . . . Trilowhat?

SIU (*off-stage*). Oh no . . .

SIU *on-stage, shaking her head.*

SIU (*on-stage*). Variety? What's that?

Paul *about to speak, but she has got it.*

No! No! I couldn't do nothing like that! What, stand up, sing 'n' dance? Speak? Front of a crowd? All of 'em, turned on me?

SIU (*off-stage*). I'd be sucked into the crowd . . .

SIU (*on-stage*). Torn to rags . . .

SIU (*off-stage*). Ripped to bits . . .

SIU (*on-stage*). I've got the same trouble as you. Crowds. I disappear into . . . other people.

What we have between us, the natural thing . . . the flow between each other, the way we wing . . .

Falters.

What we are to each other . . .

PAUL, *a sudden thought, he looks down and she catches it.*

Yes Paul, that's it! As you thought then . . . 'Like being in love'. She has your face you have hers.

PAUL. Hunh!

She points at him, angrily.

SIU (*on-stage*). Don't sneer at it! Don't sneer at being in love! It's something I can't ever have.

Distressed.

For me, it's too strong. I can't control it. He becoming her, she him . . .

SIU (*off-stage*). She him . . .

SIU (*on-stage*). Him her . . .

SIU (*off-stage*). I you . . .

SIU (*on-stage*). You I . . .

SIU (*off-stage*). Throw my voice to divert you, turn you away, turn me away . . .

PAUL, *raising the club.*

PAUL. You should be in the bin, with the key thrown away. Broadmoor. High security hospital.

SIU (*off-stage*). No. All the world is my hospital.

SIU (*on-stage*). You are my hospital.

And the on-stage SIU *takes off her face mask. It is the* MILLY *actress. With* MILLY's *characteristic gesture, she loosens her hair and shakes it free.*

SIU, *with* MILLY's *voice.*

Do you want the diamonds, Paul?

PAUL. Whatever you are . . .

SIU (*on-stage*). Don't you want the diamonds, Paul?

PAUL. Pervert, kink of nature, whatever . . .

SIU (*on-stage*). You want the daimonds, I know . . .

She throws her head right back, her throat exposed. Her hand snakes up, then fingers down, as if to plunge her hand into her gaping throat. An image of horror.

PAUL. Whatever you are! You won't get me!

He runs at her, swinging the club, two-handed. He swings it sideways, not near her. But it may as well have been – without a cry she is thrown aside by the blow, clutching the side of her head.

PAUL *stumbles onto all fours, letting go of the club. He is breathless. He catches his breath and looks at the silent figure. He crawls to her. He touches her head. He stands, looking at his hands, as if they are covered in blood.*

He is still. Then he whirls around, to where SIU *off-stage spoke.*

What? What have you to say to me?

A silence.

I'll show you! How a man can live like an animal. Free, of the lot of you!

He picks up the club. He scans the landscape. Then he runs off, bent double.

Scene Four

Blankets of bright colours. Tapestries. BRIAN huddled up. SASHA, the 'CRICKETER', and ANNETTE, the 'WHORE', watching him. SASHA taps his pads, one then the other then bends the tops of the pads.

SASHA. What do you think these things are for?

ANNETTE. What . . .

She stretches one of the suspenders out.

. . . do you think these things are for?

The suspender snaps back, stinging her.

Ow!

She licks a finger and rubs her thigh.

SASHA. When I said I'd come and work with you . . . and I'm glad to work with you, don't get me wrong . . . it's just I never thought I'd be in for dressin' up.
I mean, we're archaeologists.

ANNETTE. Archaeology's a human science . . .

SASHA. . . . Human science, yeah you keep on sayin'. But shouldn't we . . . y'know, dig the odd thing up? Bit o' spade work?

ANNETTE. We dug these clothes up. From his head.

SASHA. You think he' really . . . got this clobber on his mind?

ANNETTE. The visionary said so. And my workshop had no difficulty in making them. The visionary must be right.

SASHA. The visionary.

A disapproving sniff.

I have had most unfortunate experiences with visionaries. I spent a year in a sleeping bag in the Sahara because of one of 'em.

ANNETTE. Why?

SASHA. I got very deep into pyscho-drama theory. Too complicated t'go into.

ANNETTE. Try.

SASHA sighs.

SASHA. There's a two-thousand-year-old Arabic story. It goes . . . ready?

She nods.

'Destitute. Friendless. In a foreign land, Maruf at first mentally conceived, then described, an unbelievable caravan of riches was on its way to him. But this fantasy did not lead to his exposure, or disgrace. The imagined caravan of dreams took shape. Became, for a time, real. And arrived.

A pause.

ANNETTE. And that's what you were doing in a sleeping bag in the Sahara Desert for a year . . .

SASHA. On a visionary's advice, yup.

A pause.

ANNETTE. Well?

SASHA. Well what?

ANNETTE. Did your caravan become real, and arrive?

SASHA. Oh yeah, it arrived all right.

A pause.

Came out of the haze. Like a sailing ship. Over the sand. I nearly died.

A silence, SASHA looking away.

Well out of all that, now. Or am I? Archaeology, I thought. A little heavy diggin', I thought. Cataloguing old beer mugs 'n' doorknobs. But seeing your workin' methods, I'm not so sure.

ANNETTE, *pulling at straps on the corset.*

ANNETTE. Maybe these costumes are religious.

She means the cricket bat.

SASHA. You mean – a wand?

He waves the bat.

Yeah. Does have a holy feel. And white, for innocence? But what about you, black and red, with your arse hanging out?

ANNETTE. I could be a nun.

SASHA. A what?

ANNETTE. A bride of Christ? You are Christ, dressed in heavenly white.

SASHA. Yeah but if it's a fertility ritual, me the God you the bride, why . . . have I got my cock shut up in a cage under m' pants?

ANNETTE. Maybe it's potency. God's cock can break through anything.

SASHA. I . . . don't think we're gettin' this quite right.

BRIAN *stirs and groans.*

Hey.

ANNETTE. Here we go. Now remember what I said. He'll recognise us, if we're dressed right . . .

SASHA. If . . .

ANNETTE. Archaeologists dream of this. After years of staring at bones, bits of metal and plastic, dug out of the dirt. A conversation with someone from the past. Nervous?

SASHA. Deeply.

SASHA *and* ANNETTE *hold hands apprehensively.*

BRIAN *sits upright. He stares at them. A silence.*

ANNETTE. 'Ello, love.

BRIAN. Gor.

ANNETTE. Whatever y'want, feel free.

BRIAN. What are you?

ANNETTE. What d'you think?

BRIAN *shakes his head. He realises he is naked beneath the blankets.*

BRIAN. 'Ere! I'm starkers! What you doing to me?

ANNETTE. Anythin' you want, jus' say . . .

BRIAN. My boat come in, has it?

SASHA *and* ANNETTE *look at each other.*

SASHA. Boat?

ANNETTE. Could be a reference to Christ meetin' Peter by the shore of Lake Galilee. (*To* BRIAN.) Are you a fisher of men, dear?

She makes a move towards BRIAN, *who panics.*

BRIAN. No. Get off! Get off from me!

In a panic BRIAN *gathers the bedding about him and lurches off.*

ANNETTE. I think . . . we got it wrong.

SASHA. I think . . . human science leaves much to be desired.

ANNETTE. We did somethin' to him. But what?

SASHA. Let him go for a day or so. We'll catch up with him. Look . . . let's have a night.

They look at each other.

So, why don't you go 'n' put something sexy on?

ANNETTE. I don't fancy you.

SASHA. No? Not even dressed as a god?

He waves the bat.

ANNETTE. No.

They smile and go off hand in hand, talking.

So in the desert, how did you navigate?

SASHA. Stars. But I had the idea o' making a song-line of the journey . . .

ANNETTE. Difficult, no? Shiftin' sands?

SASHA. But not impossible, if your song-line's sung with a star map . . .

ANNETTE. I've heard of this, the Bedouin . . .

And they are gone.

Scene Five

For a few moments, the stage empty. The light shifts.

JOAN *comes on. She carries* JACE's *lathe around her neck. She puts it down and squats before it. She opens her hands, frowns, bites her lip and takes a deep breath. She puts her hands on the lathe. It does not work.*

JOAN. Damn, damn, damn!

Don't panic Joan, It is a machine, You switch it on, you switch it off.

She tries again and fails.

I do not understand. How does anything work here? I mean . . . where is the nearest Post Office? The nearest police station? Where is the town hall? Who do I complain to?

JACE comes on behind her. He stand on one foot, pivoting on a heel, curling his toes.

She turns and glares at him. He shrugs and goes off.

She stands.

There has got tobe someone in charge here. There has got to be a committee. With sub-committees. And bye-laws and policy statements and people arguing and fixing agendas, and knifing each other in the town hall. I mean, real life!

She picks the machine up.

Jace! Jace come back here. Wandering about . . . What does he do all day? Jace!

She goes off after him.

Again, for a few moments, the stage empty, the light shifting

Then three lovers – OH', LAI FUNG and SALLY come on, giggling. They carry huge, fluffy wollen capes, rugs, pillows and scarves of many colours.

They wear half-face masks.

OH'. Catch our death a' cold . . .

LAI FUNG. Cold feet?

OH'. Out a' doors? After all that rain . . .

SALLY. Yes come on . . .

LAI FUNG. Here! Go!

And they throw the capes, rugs, pillows, scarves into the air, billowing them up.

Get 'im, Sally!

SALLY. Yeah c'mon man!

LAI FUNG. Man!

SALLY. Man!

OH'. Fuckin' in the open air, this far North a' the equator? It's not healthy . . . Ow!

SALLY, *a rugby tackle on his midriff, they disappear under the pile of improvised bedding . . .*

LAI FUNG. Time to sort our married lives out!

OH'. Yeah but can't we just talk about it!

SALLY. Love in action's what we need!

OH'. Oh.

A moment. The pile of bedding still.

Right!

Yelps. The bedding bulges about. Items of clothing are thrown out.

LAI FUNG. Quiet!

SALLY. What?

The bedding pulled about, then LAI FUNG's head appears. She looks about.

OH'. What?

LAI FUNG, *retreating.*

LAI FUNG. People we don't want. Lie still!

The bedding is still. A moment, then PAUL comes on. He is very muddy. He has the club. He carries a mangled, dead rabbit.

PAUL. Three days.

And I did it.

I actually did.

Killed a fucking bunny rabbit. Shit.

He laughs, exhausted, head and shoulders sagged.

How the hell am I going to eat this thing? No! Wild man of the woods, me. I am officer material. True Stock! Born to eat raw rabbit, yup! In the back of beyond. God help me I killed her. No! No!

He straightens. His face set.

Look after the body and the mind. Get a grip.

He starts. He is alert. He looks about.

There must be a place, cave, true, deep wood, wild. For the wild man. Living hidden.

Whirls round. Eyes flitting. He scuttles off.

A moment, the bedding still. Then LAI FUNG's head appears, slowly.

LAI FUNG. All clear.

Scene Six

OH', LAI FUNG *and* SALLY *making love underneath the bedding, which humps, wriggles and moves about an area of the stage, like a huge ladybird. Grunts, laughs and whistles are heard from beneath.*

BETTY (*aside*). What clean air. I wish I had my walking shoes.

She narrows her eyes, looking into the distance.

The glory of thy world, for the simple soul, oh Lord. How beautiful it can be.

How . . . it can hover . . . before your very eyes.

Creation in its wondrous garments.

She sings quietly to herself hymn no 50 from 'Hymns And Psalms', the Methodist hymn book.

Behold the mountain of the Lord
    In latter days shall rise
On mountain tops along the hills
    And draw the wondering eyes.

A screech from the lovers. BETTY *sees them. She jolts with shock.*

SALLY. Don't do that!

OH'. Na go on!

LAI FUNG. Let me!

OH'. Ow!

SALLY. Don't!

OH'. Who is fuckin' who here!

BETTY. Oh I say, how dreadful!

She watches, transfixed.

(*Aside.*) That a body could stand so near! And they not blush!

OH'. Na, c'mon, fair do's! I am here y'know!

BETTY (*aside*). It's not true I'm against sex.

SALLY. Hold her then. For me.

BETTY (*aside*). I'm just against how sex is used.

At once, LAI FUNG'*s head pops out from the tangle of bedding.*

LAI FUNG. 'Scuse me?

BETTY. Ooh! You hussy . . . (*Aside.*)
When you look at them they have that awful look. On their skin. All this sex, it's an illness. And they always are, y'know. Sick. Dirty. Why I've got a book at home, pictures of terrible diseases . . .

LAI FUNG. How is sex used then?

BETTY (*aside*). And they have that sneer, on their lips. All the so-called libertarians have nasty lips.

LAI FUNG. 'Scuse me, you're against sex?

BETTY (*aside*). The lip, the skin. And she so young!

LAI FUNG (to SALLY). 'Ere Sally, what do you make of this woman out 'ere?

SALLY'*s head pops out.*

(*To* BETTY.) What do ya think sex should be done for, then?

BETTY. Love.

They stare at each other.

Between one man and one woman. For life.

They stare at her.

Only when married.

SALLY. What a disgustin' idea.

BETTY. Only in marriage. Within the temple. The sanctuary.

BETTY *is greatly distressed and near tears.*

SALLY. She must be one of those weirdo perverts, from New Amsterdam.

BETTY. The garden of fidelity. Private. The red rose and the white rose, the lawn, behind the hedge, safe for the children's sandpit. You've got a man under there, haven't you! I know it! Oh you young people, get married, before you ruin yourselves, get marrried before it's too late.

A silence.

SALLY. Really weird.

LAI FUNG. But I am married.

BETTY. What?

LAI FUNG. I'm married to this man.

She hits OH'*'s head, on top of the bedding.* OH', *from beneath.*

OH'. Don't do that!

SALLY. And I'm married to her.

BETTY. What?

LAI FUNG. She was married to him, under here, two years ago. And so was I.

BETTY. What?

LAI FUNG. But they had a row and broke up. Then she married me.

BETTY. What?

SALLY. But she never left him.

LAI FUNG. Yeah. I was still married to him, and now I was married to her. An' seeing as I was with both of 'em ...

SALLY. It just seemed a good idea f' the three of us, to give it another go.

LAI FUNG. Which we're doin'.

SALLY. Or trying to. We respect each other.

LAI FUNG. Yeah, we're very respectable.

OH', *from beneath the bedding.*

OH'. I've got a problem here! Massive interruptus! For cryin' out loud, someone do somethin' for me ...

SALLY. Hang on can't you? There's a woman out here. In trouble.

She shakes her self, a little wriggle to settle her clothing. A characteristic gesture.

SALLY. Come under here, with us.

LAI FUNG. Yeah come on love.

OH', *his head appearing.*

OH'. What is goin' on out here ...

LAI FUNG pushes his head back down out of sight.

SALLY (*low, to* LAI FUNG). Can you get her name?

LAI FUNG. Think so. (*To* BETTY.) Beatrice? Be-at ... Betty? Come on love. S'warm under here.

BETTY. I. Oh!

LAI FUNG. Like ... when you were a little girl? Under the bed clothes? With a light? Betty?

BETTY. Get!

BETTY *struggling, wringing her hands.*

Thee behind me!

LAI FUNG and SALLY *glance at each*

other and shrug.

SALLY. Anythin' you want, love, we're easy.

BETTY (*aside*). The light, it's going hazy. My skin, it's going shiny. Like their's.

And I do get bitter! I do! Because of my campaign against all the filth they think that I am ugly. And have no thoughts myself. No stirrings.

Desires. Oh I ...

LAI FUNG, *over her speech.*

LAI FUNG. ... You're beautiful Betty ...

BETTY. ... At home in my summer house where I work, at the bottom of the garden, behind the rambling roses, I have a collection of pornography. Under lock and key ... I tell you, the Marquis de Sade would blush at my library.

LAI FUNG. ... Don't think of yourself as ugly, Betty, why do that ...

BETTY. ... All for my work of course. To defeat the Devil, first know the Devil's ways. But late at night, my husband away, I will take out the terrible books, the vile magazines, and look at them. And not as a Christian. Not at all.

As a ... creature of nature.

SALLY. Nature? Dodgy, very dodgy. It's true the world of nature's a mirror. But it swims about in front of you. It's not fixed. It folds up, inside itself. Distances an' shapes, change. If you're going to learn from nature, it's always 'now you see it, now you don't'. We're part of the mirror, part of what we're looking into. We distort it. Nature changes with the weather, in your mind.

LAI FUNG. Sally believes in psychic weather. Isn't she sweet? C'mon.

She extends an arm to BETTY. *Then* SALLY *does.*

SALLY. Yeah, c'mon love.

OH', *from underneath.*

OH'. I hope you two know what you're doin'. Even I have a limited capacity y'know.

They ignore him.

A pause.

The two young women, each with an arm raised in invitation.

BETTY *moves towards them. Stops. Wrings her hands. Then moves another few steps.*

Then, turning away, as if talking to someone there.

BETTY. Please don't look. Please don't. Just for a minute.

LAI FUNG *and* SALLY *have not moved.* BETTY *takes the final few steps, and takes* SALLY'*s hand. She kisses it.*

And suddenly, with a shriek of laughter, the two young women pull BETTY *down under the bedding, flipping it over her head.*

Voices from underneath.

OH'. What's all this?

SALLY. Just another one!

BETTY. You wicked, wicked little thing! You wicked, wicked little thing!

SALLY. Ouch!

OH'. Dear, oh dear, oh dear!

Lights down on the heaped hump of clothes and bedding, which moves about the stage energetically.

Scene Seven

BRIAN *comes on. In a Greenlander's cloak. He carries the bedding under an arm.*

BRIAN (*aside*). Night with some . . . fuckin' weirdos. Some fucking kind of house. Took me in. Great beer 'n' all. Bit real ale-y.

He sniffs. He suddenly thinks.

Why do I tend to avoid people? 'Cos they're all after somethin'. Other people are mean sods who want you by the balls, 'n' that is that! Pass along the other side o' the street, with a can o' lager in your hand, that's my philosophy. That way you don't get hurt.

He frowns.

So, what are these weirdos after? Free bed, free meal, free beer? They got to want somethin'.

He frowns.

What do I want? I want to bowl Ian Botham for nought at the Oval. Then flatten him in the bar afterwards.

Then I want to go home to a tart with legs that are so long they go up to her armpits. Yeah. That's what Brian wants.

He shrugs.

Wantin' what you know you'll never get. It's kind o' peaceful.

He frowns.

What I really want . . . I've not ever . . . really said. Have I?

I need a drink.

That fuckin' twit in cricket gear. And his bird. I think I'll sort 'em out. And if it's free beer all round here, I am away!

He goes off.

Scene Eight

BETTY, OH', SALLY *and* LAI FUNG *have been on stage meanwhile, still beneath the pile of bedding.*

BETTY *pokes her head out.*

BETTY. Oh dear God what have I done!

OH'. I am utterly shagged dead by this woman. She just exploded. Exploded! All over me.

BETTY. Where are my clothes, give me my clothes this instant!

BETTY, *as if pulling her clothes on under the blankets.*

LAI FUNG. S'all right Betty . . .

BETTY. Take your hands off me!

BETTY *scrambles from beneath the bedding, her clothing in disarray, pulling it to rights about her. She stumbles forward on to her knees and prays.*

Jesus, don't forsake me. Don't abandon me, into their filthy hands.
Right!

She stands.

All of you! Out of there!

OH'. What now? I can't do anymore I'm utterly spent . . .

LAI FUNG. C'mon. Let's see what she's got in mind.

BETTY. Get dressed and get out of there!

SALLY. We're comin'.

The three lovers, exhausted and dishevelled, crawl out from under the bedding, pulling their clothing on, wrapping their cloaks about them.

BETTY. On your knees.

They hesitate, then kneel in a row.

Hands together!

BETTY *demonstrates. They copy her.*

OH'. Not goin' to tie our hands up now, is she?

BETTY. Eyes closed!

OH'. Dear, oh dear . . .

LAI FUNG. Sh!

BETTY. Now! Pray!

A silence. Then the three lovers shift and peek at each other. Giggles.

SALLY. What is this?

LAI FUNG. Dunno.

BETTY. No talking! Right, repeat after me! 'Lord look down upon we sinners'.

The lovers, raggedly.

LOVERS. 'Lord look down upon we sinners'.

BETTY. 'Wash us clean in Jordan's waters, cleanse our dark and sinful hearts, let us walk in light.'

The lovers pause, bewildered. Then, raggedly.

LOVERS. 'Wash us clean in Jordan's waters, cleanse our dark and sinful hearts, let us walk in light'.

BETTY. 'Amen'.

LOVERS. 'Amen'.

BETTY. Oooh!

Shakes herself.

That's better. Right! I know what Jesus wants. He has called me to found a church in this dreadful place. You are the first of millions that I will convert for Him. We will build a Church and we will start today. Come on dears!

She strides off.

SALLY. What do we do?

LAI FUNG *shrugs.*

OH'. Why do I feel that woman hasn't begun to fuck us over yet?

LAI FUNG. We'll see it as a task.

SALLY. Task?

LAI FUNG. An experiment. Can we really love this woman?

BETTY *comes back on.*

BETTY. Come on! Best foot forward, for the Lord!

She goes off.

OH'. Oh well. Let's be suckers for experience.

The lovers go off.

Scene Nine

PAUL *comes on. He is gnawing a cooked leg of the rabbit. Fur hangs from it.*

PAUL. I cooked this rabbit! And it's raw!

He throws it off-stage and backs away at once. A figure in a cloak walks on, head shaded by a large, wide brimmed hat.

You dogged me for days.

A pause.

Wales I thought. Snowdonia.

A pause.

If I do nothing else, I'll find the wilderness.

He turns. Another cloaked figure, bareheaded, comes on. PAUL stands between them.

What are you? Police?

FIRST. We were looking after Siu.

PAUL. After who?

SECOND. The woman you killed.

A pause.

PAUL. Nothing to say to you.

The SECOND figure produces a blowpipe from beneath the cloak, takes her time loading it, then uses it. PAUL clutches at his arm and swivels to face her.

FIRST. It's to slow you down, you'll be all right m'dear . . .

SECOND. But you're an ugly sod, if we're gonna get near y' . . .

FIRST. With what you done.

PAUL, *pulling at the dart in his arm.*

PAUL. Hide. Mountains. Or some . . . island.

FIRST. Not a square inch of the planet . . .

PAUL. Desert, forest . . .

SECOND. Not touched by human heel.

PAUL. Snowdonia.

The FIRST *laughs.*

FIRST. Snowdonia? S' a housing co-op. Pleasant. Bit chilly in winter.

SECOND. Siu.

FIRST. The woman you killed. She was sick.

PAUL. Nothing to say.

FIRST. We didn't know you'd do that to her. We'd have stopped y', had we known, for your sake. We apologise.

PAUL'*s knees go. He topples.*

SECOND. He's a drowning man.

PAUL. You . . . apologise . . . to me?

SECOND. That's justice.

PAUL *heavy, on all fours, slurred.*

PAUL. What are you, the hanging judges, come for me?

FIRST. Judge?

PAUL. Judging me.

SECOND. Judge y? How'd we do that?

PAUL. Condemned.

SECOND. Well you are, in't you. Condemned. Nothing we can do about that.

PAUL. To what?

They stare at him.

To what . . .

Tries to drag himself . . .

What sentence?

SECOND. He thinks he's going to be shut up. Prisoned.

FIRST. Barbaric.

PAUL. What's going to be done to me?

FIRST. That's up to you. But it'll be a terrible thing, I tell y'.

SECOND. Just remember the old story, 'bout what justice is. In an old-fashioned court. A man was found guilty o' murder.

FIRST. Yeah the judge put on a black hat, to condemn him to death.

SECOND. But the judge said 'For this murder, I condemn you to life'.

FIRST. And the man . . .

SECOND. Walked from the Court, free. Into the road outside.

FIRST. 'N killed himself.

The two 'Greenlanders' pause, then turn and sweep off the stage, quickly.

PAUL. No. Help me. Someone.

He shakes his head.

No.

He crawls away.

Scene Ten

SASHA *still dressed as the* CRICKETER *comes on, uncertainly.* BRIAN, *off.*

BRIAN. Guard! Take guard. Like I showed ya!

SASHA. Er . . . Yes.

BRIAN (*off*). This ball's soft!

SASHA. It's red though . . .

BRIAN. But it's got to be hard! If it's gonna be a cricket ball!

SASHA. Sorry, Brian. The workshop got it wrong.

BRIAN *wanders on at the side. He is dressed in cricket whites. He has a red ball in his hand.*

BRIAN (*aside*). Afternoon in Utopia. With a soft cricket ball. I begin to find that is bloody typical.

He looks at SASHA, *who is adopting a ludicrous batsman's position.* BRIAN *sighs.*

No, no, no, no!

He manhandles SASHA into position. A reasonable stance achieved.

I mean, what games do you play?

SASHA. Ball games? Football.

BRIAN. Really?

SASHA. Zen football.

BRIAN. Right. Football? Two goals.

SASHA, *puzzled.*

SASHA. No, one goal.

BRIAN. What, like a kick about? All right! One goal. Two teams.

SASHA *looks puzzled.*

BRIAN. What's a matter? Eleven-a-side. The team. The lads. Y'know, never walk alone. On f'all 'n' the rest are wankers. A fuckin' football team!

SASHA. You mean groups, playing? How can that be?

A pause. BRIAN frowning.

BRIAN. No hang about. You got one goal . . .

SASHA. Right.

BRIAN. Two players.

SASHA. Huh, huh.

BRIAN. Kickin' a ball into the goal . . . With a goalkeeper?

SASHA. No, they are their own goalkeepers.

BRIAN. Don't get it.

SASHA. It is a hard game to play.

BRIAN. Sounds it.

SASHA. Just a moment!

And he makes an immaculate practice stroke.

BRIAN. Yeah! Yeah, you caught on.

SASHA, *an elegant slow motion sweep.*

Yeah y'got it . . .

SASHA, *very excited.*

SASHA. And the ball down the other side . . .

BRIAN. Off, the off . . .

SASHA *executes a reverse sweep, in elegant slow motion.*

'Ere we go! (*Aside.*) I'll show this crapola Charlie.

BRIAN *strides off purposefully, rolling up a sleeve.*

SASHA, *to himself, under his breath.*

SASHA. Line of the ball. Concentrate. Move feet. Pitch of the ball. Follow through. Instinct. The cat.

BRIAN (*off*). This one's got your name on it mate!

A silence, SASHA poised. He makes to lift the bat. But the ball bounces on the stage and hits him in the face.

BRIAN, 'following on' from the wings wildly, leaps on to the stage with a shouted appeal.

Haaaaa izee?

SASHA *goes down covering his face with his hands.*

ANNETTE, *her clothes torn, crawls round the edge of the proscenium, huddled, hugging herself. Scratches on her skin bleed.*

On yer bike, on yer bike! Played on! Off! Off!

SASHA *gasps for air.*

Nah c'mon. It was a soft ball.

SASHA. I . . . Played it hard.

BRIAN. What?

SASHA. Like it was a hard ball.

Magician's trick here –

BRIAN *picks the ball up. He looks at it, bewildered. He drops it. It is a hard cricket ball.*

BRIAN. You people.

You take me up d'yer? I tell you! No one takes me up!

To ANNETTE.

Hey, cunt?

SASHA (*to ANNETTE*). What . . . ?

ANNETTE *shakes her head, a single jerk.* BRIAN, *panicking.*

BRIAN. Inna long grass! Back o' the jolly old cricket pavilion, what ho? Gave 'er one!

'Ey?

You asked for it, cunt! Don't tell me you did not. Stuck your fanny right up to me. Look at yer, tart!

Sorry. I'm sorry.

Looks from one to the other.

Why don't you do somethin'? I mean to me. Call the old Bill. Kick me in the goolies. Scream 'n' shout! Go on! Go on!

A silence. They are dead still.

I gotta get a drink somewhere!

He lumbers off, near tears.

A silence.

Then SASHA *pulls a glove off with his teeth. He looks at his hand. Then extends it to her. 'A question'.*

ANNETTE (*low*). No, I'm all right.

She shakes her head back.

Just because a man put his thing in me, why should I weep? A rodent. Falls in your lap.

A gesture.

Knock it away. I just . . . want a bath. Then I will make love with you. Restore.

Touching his bruised face.

SASHA. Conversation with a man from the past.

He stands, goes to her, a hand extended. She does not move.

ANNETTE. Why . . . am I dangerous to him? Why . . . is he dangerous to me?

SASHA. Dunno. What we take f'granted . . . threatens him. Things like kindness?

ANNETTE. I didn't realise.

SASHA. What?

ANNETTE. How in the past they suffered. And how it made them so ugly.

A pause.

SASHA. Come on love.

She stands. They are walking off hand-in-hand, relaxed, easy together.

ANNETTE. Summer almost done.

SASHA. Yeah, after all the rain, 'be a fine autumn. What do we do about him?

ANNETTE. He is his own problem. There's nothin' kinder to say.

They are off.

2. AUTUMN.

A vermillion and ochre stage.

Scene Eleven

The light shifts, a rainy day, an evening, a sunrise and then a fine clear sunny Autumn day. The colour of the stage changes to Autumn.

JOAN *comes on. Her clothes are now nearly entirely changed to Greenlander styles. She has the jeweller's lathe around her neck. She sets it before her and squats.*

She opens her hands. Frowns, bites her lip and takes a deep breath. She puts her hands on the lathe.

It does not work.

JOAN. Each day. Week after week.

JACE *comes on behind her. He stands with his characteristic manner, on one leg, looking at her.*

I can feel myself becoming like them. Slowing. Dreaming. I mustn't! I won't let go! I . . . (*To* JACE.) Oh, bugger off!

JACE *smiles and hops a complete turn. She sits back, closing her eyes to control her temper. Then, aside.*

I am in a world where everything I have ever dreamed of, has happened.

In here, all value is the value of labour. No one works, but everyone is busy. There are those who even love the sewers. I met some women, fanatical sewer builders. They told me they had tunnelled under the streets of what was once Los Angeles. Bendy sewers, of a plasticy stuff, earthquake proof.

How do they maintain essential services, chemical factories for basic materials? By traditions. 'Guilds' I thought, but no. You may spend two years growing tea. Just . . . get into tea growing. If you get fed up, you drift away. Build a boat, drown sailing in the Indian Ocean. But there's always tea to be had. I go mad! 'How is it organised? Production and supply?' They shrug and say 'There are enough people in the world'.

'But what' I say, 'if everyone wants to grow tea in India?'

Again, a shrug. 'There'd be a lot of tea' they say.

It can't work! There are no politics! No one decides anything! No one's in charge! I just die for . . . some authority! A little touch of leadership, a bit of bracing tyranny! God what am I saying?

JACE. You still gettin' wrong are you? 'Tween you 'n' the machine?

JOAN. I try every day. Like you said. The bloody thing must be bust!

JACE. That it?

JOAN *pauses, angry.*

JOAN. No, no, all right. That is not it. The machine is fine. It is me that is wrong.

JACE. Oh.

JOAN. As you know. But will not get angry about. You just make it work and say 'that's how'. And shrug and piss off. And stand on one leg.

JACE *scratches his crotch.*

Scratching yourself.

JACE. Right.

He continues to scratch.

JOAN. Look could you, do you think you could please stop doing that?

JACE. Oh, right.

He stops scratching. He still stands on one leg.

JOAN (*aside*). They are always there. Looking at me. Waiting for something. Blank. See through. Like ghosts. Passing through you. Some of them are really beautiful, but they shift. Yes, future ghosts, future selves . . . No personality fixed. One moment, like mental defectives, picking their noses. The next talking mathematics, or philosophy beyond anything I can fathom.

Like him. He can't even read. But he spent all the late summer, when his hand had healed, making a stone that . . .

She shakes her head, closing her eyes.

He said it was cut in seven dimensions, I looked at it. And God or the Devil or something help me, it was. And, worse for me, just for a second I saw how it was done . . . I was terrified. I found tears streaming down my face.

She opens her eyes.

Then we went down to the South Coast to throw the stone into the sea. Why? I don't know. Perhaps because he's just thick as pigshit.

JACE, *still balanced on one leg, is now picking his nose.*

Jace!

JACE *studies the bogie on his little finger. He reinserts the finger into his nostril.*

JACE. Yeah, love?

She stands and strides up to him. He is abstracted, removing the finger again and staring at it.

JOAN. Jace, now tell me. Just tell me what has happened in the last seven hundred years.

He stares at her.

JACE. What? History?

JOAN. Yes, yes.

She nods. A pause.

JACE. Well.

He laughs.

I picked m'nose.

JOAN. F' . . .

She turns away.

JACE. An' you asking me the question. That's history now.

That's why it can't work. 'Cos a history of the world would . . . itself . . . be . . . history.

JOAN. All right, sorry I asked.

JACE. Tho' . . .

He begins to scratch his crotch again.

You could have a history of the world, if it went backwards.

JOAN. All right!

But he is lost, following his train of thought.

JACE. If you could get past the first second. 'Cos you have t'prove the world didn't come into existence a second ago.

He claps his hands.

Then!

JOAN. Well it didn't did it!

JACE. Didn't it?

He smiles.

Sexy thought, eh?

You 'n' I. Just appeared.

He claps his hands, with a shout.

Now!

The smile.

Complete and beautiful.

JOAN. And you with one leg.

He looks down.

JACE. Oh dear.

JOAN, *working herself up into a rage.*

JOAN. You're like a child, or a happy dog. Infuriating, happy, stupid dog, woofing about, tongue out, you make me want to . . . Oh!

She thumps his chest with her fists, she boxes his ears. He laughs, weaving like shadow boxing, then dances away. Then he starts to box her ears in return.

Don't! Don't!

He stops, looking at her. Gravely.

JACE. Told you I weren't that bright.

A pause. Then they hold hands.

There's a man I'll take y' t' see. A fusty sod. Calls himself the last reactionary, even.

JOAN. The last reactionary?

JACE. Last on Earth, he reckons.

JOAN. Take me to him, now!

JACE. It'll be a journey, that. We'll have to kit ourselves up.

JOAN. Why, where's he live? (*Aside.*) The North Pole? With Frankenstein's monster?

JACE. In the hills. Outside Moscow.

JOAN. The Lenin Hills?

JACE. Yeah! You been there?

JOAN. Once. I went with an organisation called the Labour Party.

JACE. Oh really? What's that for, childbirth?

JOAN. Not exactly.

JACE. Severan-Severan is the man. I'll wake him up on radio. Let him know we're coming. Should be there in two months.

JOAN. Can't we drive?

JACE looks puzzled.

JOAN (*aside*). The engineering of drugs beyond anti-biotics, no cancer, no meningitis, no rheumatism, arthritis, no cholera, no schizophrenia, no AIDS, the ability to slip into six, seven, God knows what dimensions. But to build a simple combustion engine . . . That does not even occur to them. Why are the complex things easy, the simple beyond their reach?

They are going off.

JACE. We'll go through old Poland. Those Polish jewellers are crazy. They're makin' jewels out o' river silt.

JOAN. Silt?

JACE. Mud.

JOAN. Jewels out of mud. That does sound reassuringly Polish.

They are off.

Scene Twelve

BETTY *comes on. She is exhausted. Her clothing, as with* JOAN *is beginning to change. She has huge boots on, with rags tied around them, and carries, half folded, one of the asymmetrical umbrellas.*

BETTY. Heat! What have they done to Autumn? Oh, shade.

She puts the umbrella up and half collapses, half sits down.

Then she looks about, nervously.

Where are they? Oh I hope they've gone. Just for half-an-hour. Week in week out, dogging me.

But they're good, or they're very, very good. They say their prayers. I have converted three sinners!

So why do I feel . . . So fucking irritable?

A short scream.

She slaps a hand to her mouth.

And on to the stage come OH', SALLY *and* LAI FUNG, *still wearing face masks.*

SALLY. Praise the Lord!

LAI FUNG. Praised be He!

SALLY. Yea in the morning . . .

LAI FUNG. And in the evening . . .

OH'. The going down of the sun . . .

SALLY. Praise we Him.

BETTY (*sotto, aside*). Oh here they are again, oh no.

LAI FUNG. Praised be He!

OH'. For He giveth!

SALLY. He taketh away!

BETTY. Oh shut up! Shut up can't you!

A silence.

SALLY. Have we sinned, Sister Betty? If we have, tell us. In what way.

BETTY. You're . . . too bloody perfect!

LAI FUNG. And the Lord looked upon Noah and he was perfect.

SALLY. Sinless.

OH'. And the Lord looked upon Noah's wife.

SALLY. And she was perfect.

LAI FUNG. As we want to be.

SALLY. Though we know we are not.

LAI FUNG. We are sinners.

BETTY *lets the umbrella fall. She goes on all fours. She points at them.*

BETTY. I know what you are. You are my gaolers. I am in hell. And you are my keepers.

Weeping, a tiny voice. Her face to the floor.

Oh Jesus, Jesus, gentle Jesus, help me.

SALLY *makes to move towards* BETTY.

LAI FUNG *restrains her – a touch on the arm.*

OH'. Why do they think they are in hell, or in gaol? When they are at liberty?

SALLY. Maybe they like to suffer.

OH'. He don't.

He turns aside. A blitz-drunk BRIAN *staggers on. He carries a wine skin. He falls over.*

BRIAN. S'a man inna woods?

OH'. Sorry, mate?

BRIAN. All y'got's fuckin' sweet wine. S'piss! Inna woods 'ey said. Still!

LAI FUNG. Sufferin' in liberty. Seems to be the fashion this Autumn.

OH' (*to* BRIAN): You want the alcohol still? In the woods? The path's along by those houses.

BRIAN. Got ya'. Right. See ya.

OH'. Right.

BRIAN. I didn't wanna hurt her.

S'nature. S'what made me do it to her.

Too much fer a man t' bear!

He looks at them. Swaying. He looks at BETTY, *her face down on the ground.*

Thas' right, love. Eat the dirt. Thas what it's about. All about.

He staggers off.

BETTY. Oh!

She suddenly sits bolt upright.

Temptation to the brink again! So sorely, Lord.

She begins to pray fervently, lips moving.

OH'. I'm gonna give it to her.

SALLY. I don't know whether we should . . .

OH'. We got it . . .

SALLY. It'll hurt her.

OH'. She's cryin' out for it. She's been cryin' out for it f'months, while we've been taggin' along. Singing her stupid hymns.

I say give it her! Once 'n' for all. Bang.

SALLY. Violence, we don't have the right.

OH'. Well?

A pause.

SALLY. Let's do it.

They advance on BETTY, *standing around her. She opens her eyes. She flinches.*

BETTY. What are you . . . What is it?

She is frightened.

What are you going to do to me?

OH' *swings his bag from his shoulder, opens it. Puts his hand in.*

Violence! I knew what you were all along. You people. Godless. Warped.

She grabs LAI FUNG's *wrist.*

You're such a . . . pretty young thing. So lovely. Why ruin yourself, sully yourself, filthy stuff running down your sk . . . skin?

LAI FUNG *looks at her in horror and pulls her wrist away.*

OH'. We just got you this.

He takes a Bible out of his bag.

Friends scouted for it.

SALLY. Found one.

OH'. A library in Peking.

SALLY. It's been on its way to us, all Autumn. Here. Seein' you told us so many stories out of it.

OH'. Could be.

BETTY. What?

SALLY. You thought – 'The last Bible in the world'.

BETTY. The last Bible in the world?

BETTY *takes the Bible, gingerly. She holds it in her lap.*

SALLY. A present.

A silence.

Then BETTY *opens the Bible. She stares at it.*

LAI FUNG. We gotta leave you, now Betty. 'Gotta see how the children are.

BETTY. You've got chidren?

LAI FUNG. Two girls.

SALLY. They're with our other husband, in Northumberland. He wants to go off, so we're taking 'em back.

LAI FUNG. Go off fishing.

BETTY. Oh.

LAI FUNG. The children understand. They know we've been with you.

A pause.

SALLY. We tried to love you, Betty. But we don't.

OH'. No hard feelings.

BETTY *turns a page of the Bible, shakes her head unable to speak.*

Hallelujah!

SALLY. Hallelujah!

They turn and walk away.

OH' (*to* LAI FUNG). So much for the new Christian Church.

SALLY. Gonna take some time. Wash all that out of us.

SALLY *and* LAI FUNG *kiss on the mouth.* SALLY *turns and watches* BETTY *turn another page.*

Then slowly, she tears it out, throws it away. It floats over the stage.

A 'routine'. BETTY *both losing and destroying her faith, tearing 'the last Bible in the world' to pieces, laughing and crying.*

When she has done, the stage is littered with torn pages, the ripped covers.

A silence.

BETTY. What have they done to me?

De-converted me. Me!

How did they do that to me? They never said a word. They . . . gave me their love. Then took it away. And I just knew that Jesus . . . never died. And all my life, *Pilgrim's Progress*, all the prayers . . . it's fallen away.

What shall I do, without the cross to lead? What's going to become of you Betty girl, without salvation?

LAI FUNG *comes back on. She removes her mask. She played* JUDY.

BETTY *not looking at her.*

BETTY. Judy?

3.   WINTER.

A white stage.

Scene Thirteen

SEVERAN-SEVERAN *is wheeled on to the stage, fast. He is small. He has a withered arm. He is bundled up and swathed in cloaks and scarfs. Huge mittens. An elaborate 'Russian' hat. His wheelchair hangs with bags, books, boxes. Two high aerials rise from the back of the chair and whip about in the air. Flags are upon them.*

His chair is pushed by a young woman, PALACE. JOAN and JACE follow. JACE wanders about during the scene.

Everyone wears heavy winter clothing.

SEVERAN *is talking, torrentially. He has a Germanic accent. He sways and writhes in the chair as he argues, waving his arms.*

SEVERAN. We continue this confrontation in the open air. Temperature! Reading!

PALACE *consults a thermometer, that hangs from the chair.*

JOAN (*aside*). Through Poland. The plains. Rivers. Slowly, for months. The endless villages. The people on the road. As if we were not travelling at all. Everywhere a city, everywhere parkland, fields. A world that's ... enfolded in the mind, as much as there. Really they are dirt poor. And I began to understand. If we are to have a future, it will be on a planet we have wearied and worn, near to death. To live there, the future will have to be ascetic.

PALACE. Minus eleven degrees.

SEVERAN (*to* JOAN). You are disturbed by the cold?

JOAN. It's ...

SEVERAN. Good! Pain! To concentrate the analysis. What analysis? In a state of happiness? With the death of contradiction, the death of mind. As a declared reactionary, it is my function to make as much trouble as possible, in their insipid ideal. If it kills me my aim is to be the last tragedian on earth. Indeed ...

He thumps the arm-rest of the chair.

I hope it does kill me! To achieve a tragic, as opposed to an heroic death, in a society of free communistic value, that would be a victory!

PALACE (*to* JOAN). He has tried for years to shock. You mustn't let him get y'down. We love him very much.

SEVERAN *turning, waving his fists at PALACE, who, practised at this, dodges out of his reach, skilfully.*

SEVERAN. Damn passivity! Is the dialectic at rest forever? What is at war with what? Peace is senility, worst in the young! Is human nature now a mere mirror to itself? There are people abroad who believe that human nature is changed, for the good, forever. Bunk! There is a worm in man ...

PALACE. Worm in woman too? ...

SEVERAN. In the end we are all selfish, self-obsessed, with a dark heart. Human nature? It is evil and it will out.

PALACE, *angrily.*

PALACE. Ah Severan, but what human nature? The human nature of victims and slaves? Or the human nature of free men and women? Which? Tell me that, you silly old fart!

SEVERAN *roars and takes a swipe at her. She ducks.*

SEVERAN (*to* JOAN). So! On your journey did you ask your question? The last seven hundred years? What happened?

JOAN. I did, Mr Severan.

SEVERAN. And never got an answer?

JOAN. Never.

SEVERAN. Like this?

Pointing, with a jerk, over his head at PALACE.

You! Palace! Darling Simplicissima! Enlighten our guest. What has happened in the last seven centuries?

PALACE *shrugs.*

PALACE. Well. This morning ... I painted my nails.

SEVERAN. Display this major historical event!

PALACE *takes off a glove and holds out her hand for* JOAN *to inspect. Each nail is painted a different colour and glitters.*

There! She's right! That is what history has become! Painted nails!

JOAN. Amazing . . .

SEVERAN. Hologram nail varnish. Bah! Millennia of struggle! For decoration on a young woman's hand.

JOAN. Yes, but . . .

PALACE *looks directly at* JOAN. *She smiles.*

SEVERAN. Oh there is a beauty in it, yes. For that lovely little hand to glitter so, Robespierre rolled the tumbrels and ended, crouched beneath the table in the Hotel de Ville with his jaw half shot away. That, hundreds of years on, a girl may paint her nails. Is this a human wonder and a glory, or is it an historical disgrace?

JOAN (*to* PALACE). Don't get cold.

PALACE. S'all right.

She puts the glove back on.

SEVERAN. And that is the answer. For a world at peace, the only authentic history is an endless 'now'. All about me see that as liberation, freed of the past. Freed of the ravages of the old Adam! 'Liberation'! To me it is a living death. So! Was your journey pointless?

JOAN. Can y'ask that?

SEVERAN. Hunh!

A pause.

Hunh! I see you are halfway to being one of them.

He thumps the wheels of his chair with his hands.

Take me back inside! I want to sweat in the sauna! A good birching! A good scream! (*To* JOAN.) Stay in the guest house as long as you wish. (*To* PALACE.) Crack my spine! Break my neck! (*To* JOAN.) Goodbye, citizen of the past. May misery and suffering never entirely desert you, so that you remain human. Go!

JOAN (*to* PALACE). Oh God, did he . . . ?

PALACE. Yes. He mutilated himself, to live like this.

JOAN. But . . .

SEVERAN. Go! Go!

He is wheeled off, fast.

JACE. Did the great man help out, then?

JOAN. No.

JACE. What a joker, eh?

JOAN. Not really.

JACE. One o' the world's comedians, love. He's known half round the world for it.

JOAN. He wants to be tragic, he said.

JACE. Same thing for him, isn't it?

PALACE *walks back on. She stands calmly, dead still.*

PALACE. Severan is embarrassed. He has to ask me to say what he cannot.

A pause.

JOAN. Thank you.

PALACE. Of the late twentieth-century, almost nothing remains. We have more from the eleventh, the twelfth century, than we do of the twentieth.

JOAN. But . . . Libraries.

PALACE. Acid paper. We dug up two books, from sand deposits. As faint as a neolithic posthole. We think we made out one of the titles of the books.

JOAN. What was it?

PALACE. 'No Orchids For Biggles'.

JOAN. Oh no.

PALACE. Severan would like to know if it means anything to you.

JOAN. No. No. But film, Eisenstein, Fellini, Bergman . . .

PALACE. Combustible, says Severan.

JOAN. The millions of hours of TV . . .

PALACE. Electronics. Will-o'-the-wisp. Not a trace. There are bits of plastic in the archaeological record. For example, this was dug up in the Thames Valley. Could you look at it for us? We believe it is a dildo, an aid for masturbation.

PALACE *rummages in her 'Greenlander' bag. She takes out a bottle of Fairy Liquid.* JOAN *stares at it.*

A pause.

JOAN. It's a bottle of Fairy Liquid.

PALACE. Pardon?

JOAN. Put it away.

PALACE. It is not a sexual aid?

JOAN. Put it away!

JOAN *covers her face with her hands.* PALACE *puts the bottle back into her bag.*

A pause.

PALACE. Forgive me if I distress you, but that is the major artefact we have from the early lost enlightenment.

JOAN *hands away from her face.*

JOAN (*aside*). Which is what they call our time ... The early lost enlightenment.

As I talked to her, to Severan-Severan through her, I fell into mourning for my life. (*To* PALACE.) A nuclear war?

PALACE. Never was one.

JOAN. Names. (*Aside.*) I went through the US Presidents, Wilson to Reagan.

PALACE. Nixon. Yes.

JOAN. What ...

She hesitates.

What language did Nixon speak?

PALACE *shrugs.*

PALACE. Spanish, of course.

JOAN (*aside*). There remained the knowledge of the destruction of the Jews by the Nazis, but no knowledge of the First World War. No novels, no poems, three paintings by Picasso, done in his old age. Fragments of one play. I think it was *Just Between Ourselves* by Alan Ayckbourn. Severan seemed to think it was a crude, satirical reworking of Penelope, by Euripides. (*To* PALACE.) Sorry? *What* by Euripides?

PALACE. Penelope.

SEVERAN-SEVERAN *shoots on to the stage in his wheelchair, and slews to a halt. He is agitated.*

SEVERAN. From the Library of Alexandria. We have reconstructed it.

JOAN. You mean dug it up?

SEVERAN. We got the books out again.

JOAN. Dug them up ...

SEVERAN. Dug out, in a way. 153 plays by Euripides, 87 by Sophocles. Most of them pretty rough.

JOAN. You have the library of Alexandria ...

SEVERAN. The mathematics of Ajax Parocoles. Also much trivia. The autobiography of Pontius Pilate. By the way, if a paragraph in it is to be believed, Christ, was never crucified, Barrabas was. Understand!

He hits the wheels of the chair.

Enlightenment lost. Dark ages. The collapse of the West, the 'stripping' of America in the twenty-first century, interminable decades, a medievalism, out of the Soviet Union ... These writers you speak of? James Joyce? William Faulkner? Rilke, Brecht, Solzhe ... ?

JOAN. Solzhenitsyn.

SEVERAN. Struck from the record forever. In those interminable decades, brutish, censored, authoritarian. For 250 years what you call 'State Capitalism', was the iron model for Government in 'the mainland' Northern Hemisphere. North America? A garbage heap of the Third World. Do you feel the weight of it? The wasted years? The dread?

JOAN. But how, then ...

PALACE. Tyranny got tired.

SEVERAN. Hunh! History died.

PALACE. Two generations. Ninety years. Out of a second Medieval age, a new Renaissance.

SEVERAN. Bah! A way of putting it.

PALACE. There was confusion. We still study that time. To understand the forces within the movement for the beloved community. How, after the centuries, we began to talk to each other.

SEVERAN. After all the struggles, the revolutions, the human cost, the mulch, the bodies, the great ideas, mulching down ...

There never was a final revolution to give birth to this revolutionised world of theirs . . . their 'beloved community'. Bah!

PALACE. Just life after life, lived through, as best they could be lived. Ordinary life triumphed and made an extraordinary world.

SEVERAN. A mass defection! Humanity defected! Just . . . walked away! To piss in the hedges, walk in the woods, mooning about. Bah. I hate it so. Give me something to fight against, give me anguish, give me struggle! I think I'll break my arm! Someone, break my arm for me!

He huddles down in his winter clothing.

JOAN (*to* PALACE). The beloved community?

PALACE. Yes.

She shrugs.

Us.

4.   SPRING.

A yellow and green stage.

Scene Fourteen

There is a circle visible on the stage, as if grass has been scuffed away to make it.

BRIAN *comes on. He carries two improvised 'goal posts' – sticks with wooden bases, and a soft football made of cloth.*

BRIAN *puts the posts down. He raises his arms above his head. He is cheerful.*

BRIAN. Sixty-seven days without a drink. What 'n utterly horrible experience.

He bends and touches the ground. Up.

(*Aside.*) What's borin' about being dried out is that you 'ave no alternative . . . 'cept to be a really good man. Spare a thought for the poor sodding alki. No grey areas! You're a fuckin' saint or a fuckin' sinner. Sixty-seven days a saint . .

Hup!

Bends, touches the ground. Up. PAUL *comes on. He is entirely dressed as a 'Greenlander'. He has a wooden bowl. He sits down, the bowl before him.*

BRIAN *looks up from his exercises and is startled to see him.*

(*To* PAUL.) I did that, f'a bit. 'Cos of something I did.

PAUL. Don't let me . . . Embarrass you, mate.

BRIAN. You don't get me, I was a criminal. Somethin' I did.

PAUL. Ah.

BRIAN. Workin' on the roads now. Fuckin' terrible the roads round here. Still. Least y'got the right to go 'n' dig up roads, if that's what you're into.

PAUL. I . . .

He looks away.

Have to be like this for the rest of my life.

BRIAN. What did y'do?

PAUL *shakes his head. But* BRIAN *has got the thought.*

You killed her?

PAUL *startled.*

PAUL. You can do that?

BRIAN. Yeah. Dunno how. Two weeks in to gettin' off the booze . . And just like learnin' to ride a bike. First time you swim, it . . . She didn't choke, y'know.

A silence.

Mill . . . Milly? But er . . . I 'ave to tell you. She went off with another bloke . . . Graham, no . . . A Geoff.

PAUL, *suddenly his old self.*

PAUL. Geoffrey Hamish-Simpson? That little fucker? That fucking little wimp ran off with my wife?

BRIAN. Sorry.

PAUL *buries his head in his hands.*

PAUL. I've been on the road. Months. Looking for . . . the gallows.

BRIAN. Don't happen like that, does it. You've been hung. The moment you did what you did.

PAUL. Yes.

He shakes his head.

Yes.

BRIAN. Er . . .

Looks one way, then the other.

Fancy a game of footy?

PAUL *looks up.*

Or what passes for it round here. Actually, it looks impossible. But it knackers you. Right! A circle.

He scuffs round the circle on the stage.

A goal line, cuttin' the circle in half. One goal.

He puts the posts down.

On y' feet!

PAUL *stands. He shuffles into the circle.*

Stand back to back.

They do so.

That half circle in front of you, that's your area. This is mine. I can't go in yours, you can't go in mine. An' we score inta the same goal. Right?

PAUL. Ah . . .

BRIAN. You can kick off.

He plumps the ball down at PAUL's feet. He crouches, back to PAUL.

Go!

PAUL *looks down at the ball, bewildered.*

Let's be 'aving y'!

PAUL *toys with the ball. Then he suddenly moves one way. BRIAN anticipates him. PAUL, suddenly lively, switches the other way. Turns round the circle. Shoots. BRIAN stops it. They stand panting. Then BRIAN feints. PAUL finds himself wrong-footed. BRIAN swivels out of his area and scores into PAUL's side of the goal.*

Right! Again!

BRIAN *kicks off. Again BRIAN feints PAUL the wrong way and scores.*

JOAN *and JACE come on, upstage. He sets up the jeweller's lathe and works at it. After a few moments JOAN takes over. The lathe works for her. JACE stands on one leg.*

PAUL. Sod! The minds that conceived this game are fucking perverse.

BRIAN. Y'can say that again . . .

They play on.

BETTY *comes on, hand in hand with LAI FUNG, the actress who played JUDY. They are dressed in white and yellow cloaks. They are holding hands and in mid-conversation.*

BETTY. Kew Gardens . . .

LAI FUNG. A collection, like a library of plants . . .

BETTY. No, no, no, not . . . But living.

LAI FUNG. The land will be difficult, 'specially by the river. But if you get a neighbourhood to join in, they'll move the houses.

BETTY. Or we could build a big glass house.Oh! What an idea. A big hot house. A tropical climate! For folk who dream of living in the heat . . . You do meet 'em. It'll be like the old Crystal Palace. A cathedral . . .

LAI FUNG. Now Betty.

BETTY. I'm still religious dear! I just don't believe in the mucky bits anymore.

They look at each other. They embrace, kissing fully on the mouth.

The stage darkens. A rumbling sound. Like a heavy cloud passing.

It clears.

JOAN *looks up, alarmed.*

JOAN: Jace? What is it?

He does not respond. The two other 'Greenlanders' come on. They are drinking from wineskins, and merry with the drink. The 'HE/SHE' figure is one of them.

JOAN *stands, looking about her.*

1ST GREENLANDER. Brian. Have a drink.

BRIAN, *breathless from the game.*

BRIAN. Nah, I can't not ever.I'm a cripple, f'life.

1ST GREENLANDER. Nah you're stronger than that. You're just a normal bloke, Brian 'n' that's all.

BRIAN. Oh. Well.

He takes the wineskin. He drinks.

Fruits a' the earth eh?

JOAN *walking downstage. Again the darking effect, with a rumble. More pronounced.*

BRIAN *hands the wineskin back. The 'Greenlanders' turn away.*

PAUL *is staring at the 'Greenlander' who was 'SIU onstage', who makes a sign of greeting to him.*

Any of you want a game?

They do not hear him.

I said any of you want a game . . .

They cannot see him. They walk through the circle, brushing past him as if he were not there. SIU walks towards PAUL who holds out a hand. But she walks past PAUL as if he were not there.

The stage finally darkens. A roaring sound. JOAN at the end of the stage, BRIAN comes to edge.

BRIAN. Where are y'?

And they are in a repetition of the 'drowning sequence' at the end of Act One . . .

Blackout and —

Scene Fifteen

Early morning, 12 June, 1987.

Dark stage, but for the London lights.

JOAN *can just be made out, moving on her hands and knees. She is soaked.*

BILL *calling, off.*

BILL. Joan! Joan! Are you down there! Joan! Please, oh please! Joan!

JOAN, *shivering. Can hardly speak.*

JOAN. Bill?

BILL *comes on.*

BILL. Joan, oh God . . .

JOAN. There was a guy, he . . . Where is he . .

BILL. What guy?

JOAN. Off the bridge . . .

BILL. We'll get you to St Thomas's . . .

JOAN. We've got to find him!

BILL, We'll ring the coppers. Please Joan.

JOAN, *a sudden change.*

JOAN. No, it's all right. They won't let him go.

BILL. Yeah the river police . . .

JOAN. Look.

BILL. No Joan, I'll carry you . . .

JOAN. I said — look.

From her clothing she takes something, with difficulty. She holds out her fist. It is closed. She opens it. A jewel from the lathe.

BILL. What is it?

He stares.

That's . . . beautiful. Where did you get that? From the river?

JOAN *holds up the jewel above her head. A beam of light from the side of the stage hits it. Light splinters across the stage and out over the auditorium.*

Blackout.